YOUR COMPLETE SCORPIO 2025 PERSONAL HOROSCOPE

Monthly Astrological Prediction Forecast Readings of Every Zodiac Astrology Sun Star Signs- Love, Romance, Money, Finances, Career, Health, Travel, Spirituality.

Iris Quinn

Alpha Zuriel Publishing

Copyright © 2024 by **Iris Quinn**

All rights reserved. No part of this publication may be reproduced, distributed or transmitted in any form or by any means, without prior written permission.

**Alpha Zuriel Publishing
United States.**

The content contained within this book may not be reproduced, duplicated or transmitted without direct written permission from the author or the publisher.
Under no circumstances will any blame or legal responsibility be held against the publisher, or author, for any damages, reparation, or monetary loss due to the information contained within this book; either directly or indirectly.

Legal Notice:
This book is copyright protected. This book is only for personal use. You cannot amend, distribute, sell, use, quote or paraphrase any part, or the content within this book, without the consent of the author or publisher.

Disclaimer Notice:
Please note the information contained within this document is for educational and entertainment purposes only. All effort has been executed to present accurate, up to date, and reliable, complete information. No warranties of any kind are declared or implied. Readers acknowledge that the author is not engaging in the rendering of legal, financial, medical or professional advice.

Your Complete Scorpio 2025 Personal Horoscope/ Iris Quinn. -- 1st ed.

"Astrology is a language. If you understand this language, the sky speaks to you."
— IRIS QUINN

CONTENTS

SCORPIO PROFILE 1
PERSONALITY OF SCORPIO 5
WEAKNESSES OF SCORPIO 9
RELATIONSHIP COMPATIBILITY WITH
SCORPIO..13
LOVE AND PASSION 22
MARRIAGE 26
SCORPIO 2025 HOROSCOPE..............................30
   Overview Scorpio 2025 30
   January 2025 37
   February 2025 44
   March 2025 51
   April 2025 59
   May 2025 67
   June 2025 75
   July 2025 83
   August 2025 92
   September 2025 101
   October 2025..110
   November 2025 118
   December 2025 127

CHAPTER ONE

SCORPIO PROFILE

General Characteristics

- **Element:** Water
- **Quality:** Fixed
- **Ruler:** Pluto (traditional ruler: Mars)
- **Symbol:** The Scorpion
- **Dates:** October 23 - November 21

Personality Traits

- **Intense:** Experiences emotions deeply and intensely.
- **Passionate:** Invests deeply in pursuits and relationships.
- **Mysterious:** Often private and secretive about personal matters.
- **Determined:** Possesses strong willpower and perseverance.
- **Resourceful:** Skilled at finding solutions and overcoming obstacles.
- **Loyal:** Fiercely dedicated to loved ones and commitments.
- **Magnetic:** Naturally attracts others with their charismatic presence.

- **Brave:** Willing to face fears and confront challenges head-on.
- **Observant:** Notices details that others might overlook.
- **Controlling:** Prefers to maintain control over situations and outcomes.

Strengths

- **Perseverance:** Persistent and determined in achieving goals.
- **Intuition:** Highly intuitive and perceptive.
- **Loyalty:** Deeply committed and reliable in relationships.
- **Courage:** Brave and unafraid to tackle difficult situations.
- **Passion:** Brings intensity and enthusiasm to pursuits.
- **Insightfulness:** Skilled at understanding underlying truths.
- **Resilience:** Capable of bouncing back from setbacks.

Weaknesses

- **Jealousy:** Can be prone to feelings of jealousy and possessiveness.
- **Secretive:** Often keeps thoughts and feelings hidden.
- **Control Issues:** Tends to be overly controlling or manipulative.
- **Stubbornness:** May be inflexible and resistant to change.
- **Obsessiveness:** Can become fixated on certain ideas or goals.

- **Suspicion:** Naturally suspicious and distrustful.

Planets and Their Influences

- **Career Planet:** Saturn – Provides discipline and structure in professional life.
- **Love Planet:** Venus – Governs affection, beauty, and romantic relationships.
- **Money Planet:** Jupiter – Influences financial matters and abundance.
- **Planet of Fun, Entertainment, Creativity, and Speculations:** Neptune – Encourages dreams and imagination.
- **Planet of Health and Work:** Mars – Influences drive, energy, and work ethic.
- **Planet of Home and Family Life:** Moon – Governs emotions and domestic affairs.
- **Planet of Spirituality:** Pluto – Represents transformation, rebirth, and deep insight.
- **Planet of Travel, Education, Religion, and Philosophy:** Mercury – Governs communication and learning.

Compatibility

- **Signs of Greatest Overall Compatibility:** Cancer, Pisces
- **Signs of Greatest Overall Incompatibility:** Leo, Aquarius
- **Sign Most Supportive for Career Advancement:** Capricorn
- **Sign Most Supportive for Emotional Well-being:** Cancer
- **Sign Most Supportive Financially:** Taurus

- **Sign Best for Marriage and/or Partnerships:** Taurus
- **Sign Most Supportive for Creative Projects:** Pisces
- **Best Sign to Have Fun With:** Sagittarius
- **Signs Most Supportive in Spiritual Matters:** Pisces
- **Best Day of the Week:** Tuesday

Additional Details

- **Colors:** Black, Deep Red
- **Gem:** Topaz
- **Scent:** Patchouli, Cedarwood
- **Birthstone:** Topaz
- **Quality:** Fixed (steadfast and determined)

PERSONALITY OF SCORPIO

Scorpio, born between October 23 and November 21, is a water sign ruled by Pluto, the planet of transformation, and Mars, the traditional ruler of intensity and action. This unique combination of planetary influences shapes the Scorpio personality into one of the most complex and intriguing of the zodiac. Deep, intense, and often mysterious, Scorpios navigate life with a level of emotional and intellectual depth that sets them apart.

At the core of a Scorpio's personality is their intensity. They approach life with a fervor that is unparalleled, diving deep into their emotions and experiences. This intensity is evident in everything they do, whether it's their work, relationships, or personal pursuits. Scorpios do not believe in doing things halfway; they are all or nothing. This can make them incredibly passionate and committed, but it can also lead to an all-consuming focus on their goals and desires.

Scorpios are known for their keen intuition and perceptive nature. They have an uncanny ability to read people and situations, often seeing through facades to the underlying truth. This perceptiveness makes them excellent judges of character and gives them an edge in navigating complex social dynamics. They trust their gut feelings and are rarely wrong, which can sometimes make them seem almost psychic to those around them.

The emotional depth of Scorpios is another defining characteristic. They experience emotions with great intensity and are not afraid to confront the darker aspects of their psyche. This willingness to delve into their own and others' emotional landscapes gives them a profound understanding of human nature. However, this depth can also make them susceptible to emotional turmoil, as they feel everything so deeply. It is not uncommon for Scorpios to experience extreme highs and lows, which they navigate with their characteristic resilience and strength.

In relationships, Scorpios are fiercely loyal and protective. They form deep bonds with their loved ones and are unwavering in their commitment. This loyalty is a double-edged sword; while it ensures they are reliable and devoted partners, it can also lead to possessiveness and jealousy. Scorpios have a strong desire to maintain control over their relationships, and they can become suspicious if they feel their trust is being betrayed. It is crucial for their partners to understand and respect this need for loyalty and transparency.

Scorpios are also known for their resourcefulness and determination. When they set their sights on a goal, they pursue it with relentless focus and tenacity. They are not easily deterred by obstacles and often find creative solutions to overcome challenges. This resourcefulness extends to all areas of their lives, making them adept problem-solvers who can navigate even the most complex situations with ease.

Despite their many strengths, Scorpios can also be prone to certain weaknesses. Their intensity and desire for control can sometimes make them seem manipulative or domineering. They have a tendency to hold grudges and can be unforgiving if they feel wronged. Their suspicion and jealousy can also strain relationships, as they struggle to trust completely. It is important for Scorpios to work on balancing their intense emotions and learning to let go of past hurts to foster healthier connections with others.

Scorpios are deeply introspective and constantly seek to understand themselves and the world around them. This introspection can lead them to profound personal growth and transformation. They are not afraid to confront their flaws and work on self-improvement, which is a testament to their resilience and inner strength. This transformative nature is one of their most powerful attributes, as they are constantly evolving and striving to become the best versions of themselves.

In conclusion, the personality of a Scorpio is marked by intensity, emotional depth, intuition, and determination. They are passionate and loyal individuals who approach life with a fervor that is unmatched. While their need for control and their susceptibility to jealousy can present challenges, their resilience and resourcefulness enable them to overcome obstacles and achieve their goals. Scorpios are complex and multifaceted, with a profound understanding of human nature and a relentless drive for personal growth and transformation. Their presence is magnetic, drawing others in with their charisma and unwavering commitment to living life to the fullest.

WEAKNESSES OF SCORPIO

Scorpio, while known for their intensity and depth, also possesses several weaknesses that can pose challenges in their personal and professional lives. One of the most significant weaknesses of Scorpio is their tendency towards jealousy and possessiveness. This stems from their deep emotional investment in their relationships and their desire for control. Scorpios feel intensely and form profound attachments to the people they care about, which can lead to a fear of betrayal or loss. This fear often manifests as jealousy, as they constantly seek reassurance of their partner's loyalty. While their devotion is commendable, it can create tension and mistrust if not managed properly. Scorpios must learn to trust and allow their partners some freedom, understanding that love cannot be controlled or demanded.

Another notable weakness of Scorpio is their inclination towards secrecy and manipulation. Scorpios are naturally private and guard their emotions closely. They often prefer to keep their true feelings hidden, revealing only what they choose to share. While this can give them an air of mystery, it can also lead to misunderstandings and a lack of transparency in their relationships. Additionally, their desire for control can drive them to manipulate situations or people to achieve their desired outcomes. This manipulative tendency can be detrimental, leading to strained relationships and a lack of trust from others. Scorpios need to practice openness and honesty, recognizing that vulnerability can strengthen connections rather than weaken them.

Scorpios are also prone to holding grudges and being unforgiving. Their intense nature means they feel deeply, and when they are wronged, they find it difficult to let go. They may harbor resentment for long periods, which can poison their relationships and their own peace of mind. This inability to forgive can create a cycle of bitterness and retaliation, preventing them from moving forward and finding closure. It is essential for Scorpios to learn the value of forgiveness and the importance of releasing past hurts to foster healthier, more positive interactions.

Another challenge for Scorpios is their susceptibility to obsessive behavior. When they set their sights on a goal or become fixated on an idea, they can become consumed by it. This single-minded determination can be a double-edged sword; while it drives them to achieve great things, it can also lead to burnout and an inability to see the bigger picture. Scorpios may neglect other important aspects of their lives in their pursuit of a singular objective, which can cause imbalances and lead to personal and professional setbacks. Finding a balance and learning to diversify their focus is crucial for maintaining overall well-being and achieving sustainable success.

Scorpios' intense emotional nature can also make them prone to mood swings and emotional extremes. They can go from passionate highs to despairing lows, often experiencing a tumultuous internal landscape. This emotional volatility can be challenging for their loved ones to navigate and can lead to instability in their relationships. Scorpios need to develop healthy coping mechanisms to manage their emotions and seek support when needed. Practicing mindfulness and emotional regulation can help them maintain a more balanced and stable emotional state.

Lastly, Scorpios can be highly suspicious and distrustful. Their perceptive nature makes them acutely aware of potential threats or deceptions, but this can also lead them to see betrayal where there is none. Their suspicion can create barriers in their relationships, as their partners may feel constantly scrutinized or mistrusted. Building trust and learning to give people the benefit of the doubt is essential for Scorpios to cultivate healthy, trusting relationships. They need to recognize that not everyone has ulterior motives and that trust is a cornerstone of any strong, enduring connection.

In conclusion, while Scorpios possess many strengths, their weaknesses can pose significant challenges. Their jealousy, secrecy, unforgiving nature, obsession, emotional volatility, and suspicion can create obstacles in their personal and professional lives. By acknowledging these weaknesses and working towards addressing them, Scorpios can foster healthier relationships and achieve greater personal growth. Embracing trust, forgiveness, and emotional balance will enable them to harness their intensity and depth in positive, constructive ways, leading to a more fulfilling and harmonious life.

RELATIONSHIP COMPATIBILITY WITH SCORPIO

Based only on their Sun signs, this is how Scorpio interacts with others. These are the compatibility interpretations for all 12 potential Scorpio combinations. This is a limited and insufficient method of determining compatibility.

However, Sun-sign compatibility remains the foundation for overall harmony in a relationship.

The general rule is that yin and yang do not get along. Yin complements yin, and yang complements yang. While yin and yang partnerships can be successful, they require more effort. Earth and water zodiac signs are both Yin. Yang is represented by the fire and air zodiac signs.

Scorpio with Yang Signs (Fire and Air)

Scorpio and Aries (Yang with Yin):

Scorpio and Aries have a relationship filled with intensity and passion. Both signs are strong-willed, determined, and possess a deep emotional connection, which can create a powerful and transformative bond. Aries is drawn to Scorpio's mysterious and intense nature, while Scorpio appreciates Aries' courage and straightforwardness. However, their mutual desire for control and dominance can lead to power struggles and conflicts. To make this relationship work, they need to be mindful of their tempers, learn to compromise, and respect each other's strengths. When they work together, they can achieve great things and create a deeply fulfilling and passionate relationship.

Scorpio and Leo (Yang with Yin):

Scorpio and Leo are both powerful signs that can create a dynamic and magnetic relationship. Leo's charisma and confidence complement Scorpio's depth and intensity. They both appreciate loyalty and can form a strong bond based on mutual respect and admiration. However, their strong personalities can lead to conflicts, as both want to be in control. To make this relationship work, they need to learn to balance their egos and work together as a team. Communication and understanding are essential for maintaining harmony and avoiding power struggles.

Scorpio and Sagittarius (Yang with Yin):

Scorpio and Sagittarius have very different approaches to life, which can create both challenges and opportunities for growth. Sagittarius' adventurous and freedom-loving nature contrasts with Scorpio's deep emotional intensity and desire for control. While Scorpio can provide depth and emotional connection, Sagittarius offers excitement and new experiences. They can learn a lot from each other, but they need to respect their differences and allow each other the space to be themselves. Patience, understanding, and a willingness to compromise are essential for making this pairing work.

Scorpio and Gemini (Yang with Yin):

The relationship between Scorpio and Gemini is lively and intellectually stimulating. Gemini's curiosity and adaptability complement Scorpio's depth and intensity. They enjoy a mentally engaging partnership where boredom rarely sets in, thanks to Gemini's versatile nature and Scorpio's drive for emotional connection. Scorpio can sometimes be frustrated by Gemini's indecisiveness, while Gemini may find Scorpio too intense. To make this pairing work, they need to appreciate each other's strengths—Gemini's communicative skills and Scorpio's emotional depth—and find a balance between flexibility and stability.

Scorpio and Libra (Yang with Yin):

Scorpio and Libra, being neighboring signs, create a dynamic and balanced relationship. Libra's charm, diplomacy, and love for harmony complement Scorpio's intensity and emotional depth. Libra can help Scorpio see different perspectives and create balance, while Scorpio adds passion and intensity to Libra's life. Their relationship thrives on the attraction of opposites, but Scorpio's directness can sometimes clash with Libra's desire for peace, leading to occasional conflicts. Communication and understanding are essential for maintaining harmony. By learning to appreciate their differences, they can create a harmonious and fulfilling partnership.

Scorpio and Aquarius (Yang with Yin):

Scorpio and Aquarius share a love for independence, innovation, and intellectual stimulation. Aquarius' visionary ideas and unconventional approach to life attract Scorpio, who admires their originality and intellect. Scorpio's emotional depth and intensity complement Aquarius' forward-thinking nature, creating a relationship that is both exciting and intellectually stimulating. They enjoy exploring new ideas and experiences together, keeping their relationship fresh and dynamic. However, both signs value their freedom, which can sometimes lead to a lack of emotional closeness. They need to work on maintaining a strong emotional connection while respecting each other's need for independence.

Scorpio with Yin Signs (Earth and Water)

Scorpio and Taurus (Yin with Yin):

Scorpio and Taurus, being opposite signs, can create a deeply rooted and passionate relationship. Taurus' steadiness and reliability provide a solid foundation for Scorpio's emotional depth and intensity. Both signs value loyalty and are committed to building a secure and lasting partnership. However, their stubbornness can lead to conflicts if neither is willing to compromise. To make this relationship work, they need to learn to appreciate each other's strengths and be willing to make sacrifices for the sake of harmony. Their differences can complement each other, creating a balanced and enriching partnership.

Scorpio and Virgo (Yin with Yin):

Scorpio and Virgo have complementary qualities that can create a harmonious and supportive relationship. Virgo's analytical and methodical nature contrasts with Scorpio's emotional intensity and intuition. While Virgo brings practicality and attention to detail to Scorpio's life, Scorpio offers Virgo emotional depth and insight. Their differences can lead to misunderstandings, but if they learn to appreciate and balance each other's strengths, they can create a complementary and enriching partnership. Patience, understanding, and a willingness to compromise are essential for making this pairing work.

Scorpio and Capricorn (Yin with Yin):

Scorpio and Capricorn share a strong sense of determination and ambition, which can create a powerful and goal-oriented relationship. Capricorn's disciplined and structured approach to life complements Scorpio's emotional depth and intensity. They both value loyalty and are committed to building a secure and lasting partnership. However, their strong personalities can lead to conflicts if neither is willing to compromise. To make this relationship work, they need to appreciate each other's strengths and work together as a team. Communication and understanding are essential for maintaining harmony and avoiding power struggles.

Scorpio and Cancer (Yin with Yin):

Scorpio and Cancer have a natural affinity for each other, creating a deeply emotional and nurturing relationship. Both signs are highly intuitive and value emotional connection and loyalty. Scorpio's intensity and passion complement Cancer's sensitivity and nurturing nature. They understand each other's emotional needs and can provide the support and care that both crave. However, Scorpio's intensity can sometimes overwhelm Cancer, leading to conflicts. To make this relationship work, they need to communicate openly and create a safe space for each other's emotions. Mutual understanding and respect are essential for maintaining harmony.

Scorpio and Scorpio (Yin with Yin):

When two Scorpios come together, the relationship is intense, passionate, and transformative. Both partners share a deep emotional connection and a desire for loyalty and commitment. They understand each other's need for intensity and can create a powerful bond based on mutual respect and admiration. However, their similar traits can lead to frequent clashes, as both can be stubborn and possessive. To make this relationship work, they need to learn patience, compromise, and how to balance their competitive natures. Communication and mutual respect are key to maintaining harmony.

Scorpio and Pisces (Yin with Yin):

Scorpio and Pisces share a deep emotional connection and a natural affinity for each other. Pisces' gentle, introspective, and emotional nature complements Scorpio's intensity and passion. While Scorpio provides emotional depth and intensity, Pisces offers compassion, creativity, and a sense of spirituality. They understand each other's emotional needs and can provide the support and care that both crave. However, Scorpio's intensity can sometimes overwhelm Pisces, leading to misunderstandings. To make this relationship work, they need to communicate openly and create a safe space for each other's emotions. Mutual understanding and respect are essential for maintaining harmony.

In conclusion, Scorpio's compatibility with other sun signs varies widely based on the yin and yang theory. Water and earth signs generally complement Scorpio's intense and emotional nature, leading to deep and meaningful relationships. Fire and air signs, while presenting more challenges, can provide excitement and intellectual stimulation, requiring more effort to navigate their differences. With mutual respect, understanding, and a willingness to learn from each other, Scorpio can form successful and fulfilling partnerships with any sign.

LOVE AND PASSION

Scorpio, ruled by Pluto and Mars, embodies a level of intensity in love and passion that is unparalleled in the zodiac. Their approach to relationships is all-encompassing, marked by a depth of feeling and a willingness to explore the full spectrum of emotional experiences. For Scorpio, love is not just a fleeting emotion but a profound journey that intertwines their soul with that of their partner. They seek connections that are not only physically satisfying but also emotionally and spiritually enriching.

Scorpios are often drawn to the mysteries of life, and this curiosity extends to their romantic relationships. They are naturally inquisitive and desire to understand their partners on a deep level. This quest for knowledge about their partner's inner world makes them highly perceptive and intuitive lovers. They can often sense their partner's needs and desires before they are even spoken, which creates a bond that feels almost telepathic. This intuitive connection fosters a level of intimacy that is deeply fulfilling for both partners.

In matters of passion, Scorpios are intensely sensual. They approach physical intimacy with a fervor that reflects their overall approach to life—wholehearted and unreserved. For Scorpio, passion is an essential component of a relationship, and they seek to merge with their partner on a physical level as much as on an emotional one. This merging is not merely about physical pleasure but about creating a powerful connection that transcends the ordinary. Scorpios bring a level of dedication and focus to their intimate encounters that can be incredibly rewarding for their partners.

However, the intensity of Scorpio's love and passion also comes with challenges. Their deep emotional investment in relationships means they can be prone to jealousy and possessiveness. When Scorpios love, they love completely, and the thought of losing their partner or being betrayed can be devastating. This fear can sometimes lead them to be overly protective or controlling. It is crucial for Scorpios to find a balance between their intense need for security and their partner's need for freedom and trust. Open communication and mutual reassurance are key to maintaining a healthy dynamic where both partners feel valued and respected.

Scorpios also have a tendency to be secretive, even in relationships. While they crave deep emotional connections, they often guard their own feelings closely. This secrecy can create barriers and misunderstandings if their partner feels shut out or unable to reach the true depths of their emotions. Scorpios must learn to open up and share their vulnerabilities, understanding that true intimacy is built on transparency and mutual trust. By allowing themselves to be seen and understood, they can forge even stronger and more resilient connections.

Despite their intensity, Scorpios are incredibly loyal and dedicated partners. Once they commit, they are in it for the long haul. They will go to great lengths to protect and support their loved ones, often putting their partner's needs above their own. This loyalty creates a stable foundation for the relationship, as their partners can always count on their unwavering support. However, Scorpios must also ensure that their devotion does not lead to self-neglect. It is important for them to maintain a sense of individuality and self-care, even within the context of a deeply committed relationship.

Another aspect of Scorpio's love life is their need for transformation and growth. Scorpios are constantly evolving, and they seek relationships that allow for this continuous personal and mutual development. They are drawn to partners who challenge them, who push them to explore new facets of themselves, and who are not afraid to delve into the depths of their own psyches.

This quest for growth can lead to a powerful and dynamic relationship where both partners feel continually inspired and invigorated.

In summary, love and passion for Scorpio are intense, profound, and transformative. They approach relationships with an all-consuming fervor, seeking deep emotional and physical connections that go beyond the superficial. While their intensity can sometimes lead to challenges such as jealousy and secrecy, their loyalty, dedication, and desire for deep intimacy make them incredibly rewarding partners. By embracing openness, balancing their need for security with trust, and fostering mutual growth, Scorpios can create powerful and enduring relationships that are as fulfilling as they are passionate.

MARRIAGE

Marriage for Scorpio is a profound and transformative journey, one that requires both partners to engage deeply and authentically. Scorpios approach marriage with the same intensity and passion that characterize their overall demeanor. They seek a union that is not only emotionally and physically fulfilling but also spiritually and intellectually stimulating. For Scorpio, marriage is a sacred bond, a partnership where trust, loyalty, and deep emotional connection are paramount.

To keep a Scorpio happy in marriage, it is essential to understand their need for depth and authenticity. Scorpios crave honesty and transparency. They are perceptive and intuitive, often sensing when something is amiss, so any attempt to deceive or withhold information can be detrimental. Open and honest communication is the cornerstone of a successful marriage with Scorpio. They appreciate partners who are willing to share their innermost thoughts and feelings, creating a space where both can explore their emotional landscapes without fear of judgment or rejection. This level of honesty fosters a sense of security and trust that is crucial for Scorpio's well-being in a marriage.

Scorpio men in marriage are fiercely loyal and protective of their partners. They take their role as a husband seriously, often going above and beyond to ensure their spouse feels loved, valued, and supported. A Scorpio man brings a deep sense of commitment and dedication to the relationship. He is driven by a desire to create a strong and stable home life. To keep a Scorpio man happy in marriage, it is important to recognize and appreciate his efforts. He thrives on feeling needed and valued, so expressing gratitude and acknowledging his contributions can strengthen the bond. Scorpio men also appreciate a partner who is willing to explore life's mysteries with them, whether through intellectual pursuits, spiritual growth, or shared adventures.

Scorpio women in marriage bring a blend of passion, intuition, and nurturing. They are deeply committed to their partners and often take on the role of the emotional anchor in the relationship. A Scorpio woman is fiercely protective of her loved ones and will do whatever it takes to ensure their happiness and security. To keep a Scorpio woman happy in marriage, it is crucial to provide emotional support and validation. She needs to feel that her partner is equally invested in the relationship and is willing to delve into deep emotional waters. Acknowledging her intuitive insights and respecting her need for emotional depth can create a fulfilling and balanced partnership.

The secret to making a marriage with Scorpio work lies in embracing the intensity and depth that they bring to the relationship. Scorpios need to feel a profound connection with their partner, one that goes beyond the surface level. This means being willing to engage in deep conversations, exploring each other's dreams, fears, and aspirations. It also means being open to the transformative nature of the relationship. Scorpios are constantly evolving and seek partners who are willing to grow and change alongside them. This mutual commitment to personal and relational growth can create a dynamic and fulfilling marriage.

Another key aspect of a successful marriage with Scorpio is trust. Scorpios value loyalty and fidelity above all else. Any breach of trust can be devastating and difficult to repair. It is essential to build and maintain trust through consistent honesty, reliability, and emotional transparency. This creates a safe space where Scorpio feels secure and able to fully invest in the relationship.

In addition to trust and emotional depth, maintaining a sense of passion and excitement is crucial for keeping Scorpio happy in marriage.

Scorpios are passionate beings who thrive on intensity and excitement. Finding ways to keep the spark alive, whether through romantic gestures, shared adventures, or exploring new interests together, can help sustain the emotional and physical connection. Scorpios appreciate partners who are willing to dive into new experiences and keep the relationship vibrant and dynamic.

Ultimately, a successful marriage with Scorpio requires a willingness to engage deeply, embrace transformation, and build a foundation of trust and loyalty. By understanding and honoring Scorpio's need for depth, authenticity, and passion, both partners can create a powerful and enduring union that is as emotionally fulfilling as it is transformative. Through mutual respect, open communication, and a shared commitment to growth, marriage with a Scorpio can be a deeply rewarding and life-changing experience.

CHAPTER TWO

SCORPIO 2025 HOROSCOPE

Overview Scorpio 2025

Scorpio (October 23 - November 21)

2025 is shaping up to be a transformative and empowering year for those born under the sign of Scorpio. As the celestial bodies weave their intricate dance, they will bring a mix of intense experiences, profound insights, and opportunities for growth and metamorphosis. Buckle up, Scorpio, because this year is going to be a wild ride!

The year kicks off with a powerful focus on your 3rd house of communication, learning, and local community. With Mars, your traditional ruling planet, spending an extended period in this sector, you'll be fired up and ready to speak your truth, learn new skills, and make your mark on the world around you. This is a fantastic time to take a course, start a blog, or get involved in your local community. Just be mindful of potential conflicts or misunderstandings, as Mars can sometimes bring a bit of a "my way or the highway" attitude.

But wait, there's more! In mid-January, Uranus, the planet of sudden change and innovation, will turn direct in your 7th house of partnerships. This could bring some exciting and unexpected developments in your closest relationships, whether romantic, business, or platonic. Be open to new ways of relating and collaborating, and don't be afraid to let go of connections that are no longer serving your highest good.

As the year progresses, a major shift occurs in March when Saturn, the planet of structure and responsibility, moves into your 6th house of health, work, and daily routines. This transit, which will last until 2025, is an opportunity to get serious about your well-being and your work life. It's time to establish healthy habits, set clear boundaries, and take charge of your schedule. Yes, it may require some discipline and hard work, but the rewards will be well worth it in the long run.

The Aries New Moon on March 29 falls in your 6th house, bringing a powerful opportunity to set intentions around your health, work, and daily habits. This is a great time to start a new exercise routine, revamp your diet, or tackle that big project at work. Just be sure to pace yourself and don't take on more than you can handle.

In mid-April, Jupiter, the planet of expansion and growth, will form a square aspect to Pluto, your modern ruling planet, in your 3rd house. This could bring some intense and transformative experiences related to communication, learning, or travel. You may find yourself questioning long-held beliefs or confronting hidden truths. Trust in the process of growth and evolution, even if it feels uncomfortable at times.

As the year progresses, the North Node, a point of destiny and soul growth, will shift into your 7th house of partnerships, while the South Node will move into your 1st house of self and identity. This suggests a powerful opportunity to learn and grow through your relationships with others, while also letting go of old patterns of self-reliance and independence. It's time to embrace vulnerability, intimacy, and collaboration, even if it feels scary at times.

In late April, Pluto will turn retrograde in your 3rd house, bringing a period of deep reflection and internal processing related to your thoughts, beliefs, and communication style. This is a time to dig deep and confront any fears, shadows, or limiting patterns that may be holding you back. Trust in the power of introspection and self-awareness to guide you towards greater clarity and authenticity.

The mid-year period brings a series of powerful eclipses that will accelerate your growth and transformation. The Total Lunar Eclipse in Virgo on March 14 will highlight the need for balance and integration between your individuality and your relationships. This is a time to assess the give-and-take in your partnerships and to make any necessary adjustments. The Partial Solar Eclipse in Aries on March 29 will bring a powerful opportunity to set intentions around your health, work, and daily routines. Trust your instincts and take bold action towards your goals.

In mid-June, Saturn will briefly shift into your 5th house of creativity, self-expression, and romance, giving you a preview of the growth and challenges to come in these areas. This is a time to take stock of your creative pursuits and your love life, and to start putting in place the structures and boundaries needed for long-term success and fulfillment.

The second half of the year brings a focus on your inner world, spirituality, and emotional healing. Jupiter, the planet of expansion and growth, will spend an extended period in your 8th house of deep transformation, intimacy, and shared resources. This is a powerful time for personal growth, therapy, and facing your deepest fears and desires. Trust in the process of death and rebirth, and know that the universe is supporting you every step of the way.

In late September, Mars, your traditional ruling planet, will shift into your 1st house of self and identity, bringing a surge of energy, confidence, and assertiveness. This is a fantastic time to take bold action towards your goals, to assert your needs and desires, and to make your mark on the world. Just be mindful of potential conflicts or power struggles, and strive to find a balance between your own needs and the needs of others.

The Partial Solar Eclipse in Virgo on September 21 will bring a powerful opportunity for healing and transformation in your 11th house of friendships, groups, and community. This is a time to let go of any toxic or draining social connections, and to embrace a more authentic and supportive network of like-minded individuals. Trust in the power of vulnerability and shared humanity to guide you towards greater connection and belonging.

As the year comes to a close, Jupiter will turn direct in your 8th house, bringing a sense of hope, faith, and optimism to your deepest emotional and spiritual journey. This is a time to trust in the process of growth and transformation, to embrace the unknown, and to have faith in your own resilience and strength. Know that the challenges and struggles you've faced this year have ultimately been serving your highest good and evolution.

Throughout the year, the influence of Neptune in your 5th house of creativity, romance, and self-expression will continue to bring a sense of magic, inspiration, and unconditional love to these areas of your life. This is a beautiful time to tap into your imagination, to express your unique talents and gifts, and to open your heart to the beauty and wonder of the world around you. Trust in the power of creativity and love to heal, transform, and uplift you.

In December, Venus will join Pluto in your 3rd house, intensifying your desire for deep, honest communication and intellectual stimulation in your relationships. The Capricorn New Moon on December

19 will bring a powerful opportunity to set intentions around your communication skills, learning, and local community involvement.

Overall, 2025 is a year of profound growth, transformation, and self-discovery for Scorpio. With Saturn and the eclipses bringing challenges and opportunities for discipline, responsibility, and emotional healing, and with Jupiter and Neptune bringing expansion, faith, and creativity, this is a time to embrace your deepest truths and your highest potential. Trust in the journey, stay true to yourself, and know that the universe is guiding you towards your ultimate destiny. With an open heart, a curious mind, and a willingness to face your fears, you have the power to create a life of profound meaning, love, and purpose. Here's to an incredible 2025, Scorpio!

January 2025

Overview Horoscope for the Month:

Scorpio, January 2025 is a month of profound transformation and new beginnings. As the year kicks off, you'll feel a powerful urge to shed old skin and embrace a new version of yourself. The celestial energies are aligned to support your growth and evolution, but it won't always be a smooth ride. Prepare for some intense soul-searching, deep healing, and major breakthroughs. Trust the journey and know that you are exactly where you need to be.

The month starts with a bang as Vesta, the asteroid of devotion and sacred service, enters your sign on January 2nd. This transit will amplify your natural intensity and passion, and call you to dedicate yourself to a higher purpose or cause. You may find yourself feeling more focused, disciplined, and committed to your goals and values. Use this energy to fuel your ambition and make a positive impact in the world.

On January 6th, Mars, your traditional ruling planet, stations retrograde in Cancer, your 9th house of travel, higher education, and spiritual growth. This transit, which lasts until February 23rd, will bring a period of reflection and re-evaluation around your beliefs, philosophies, and long-term goals. You may find yourself questioning your path or seeking a deeper meaning and purpose in life. Be open to new perspectives and insights, and trust that the universe is guiding you towards your highest truth.

The Full Moon in Cancer on January 13th will bring a powerful culmination or turning point in your spiritual journey or educational pursuits. You may receive important news or opportunities related to travel, publishing, or higher learning. Trust your intuition and be willing to take a leap of faith towards your dreams. Remember that growth often requires stepping outside your comfort zone.

Love:

In love, January 2025 is a month of deep intimacy, vulnerability, and emotional healing. With Venus, the planet of love and relationships, entering sensitive Pisces on January 2nd, you'll be craving a soul-level connection with your partner or seeking a relationship that transcends the physical realm. This is a time to open your heart, express your deepest feelings and desires, and create a safe space for love to flourish.

If you're in a committed relationship, take time to nurture your bond through shared activities that bring you closer together, such as a romantic getaway, couples' therapy, or spiritual practice. Be willing to be vulnerable and transparent about your fears, wounds, and dreams, and trust in the healing power of love and intimacy. Remember that true love requires both partners to show up fully and authentically.

If you're single, you may find yourself attracted to people who share your depth, intensity, and spiritual values. Look for partners who are willing to do the inner work of growth and transformation, and who appreciate your unique qualities and strengths. Trust your intuition and let your heart guide you towards meaningful connections. Remember that the most important relationship is the one you have with yourself.

Career:
In your career, January 2025 is a month of powerful new beginnings and opportunities for growth. With the New Moon in Aquarius on January 29th falling in your 4th house of home and family, you may be considering a major career change or relocating for work. Trust that the universe is guiding you towards your highest potential and purpose, even if the path is not always clear or easy.

Take time to reflect on your long-term goals and values, and make sure that your work aligns with your authentic self and soul's calling. If you're feeling unfulfilled or stuck in your current job, consider exploring new options or seeking out mentors who can support you in your professional development. Remember that your work is a reflection of your inner world, and that you have the power to create a career that brings you joy, fulfillment, and abundance.

Finances:

In finances, January 2025 is a month of unexpected windfalls and opportunities for growth. With Uranus, the planet of sudden change and innovation, turning direct in your 7th house of partnerships on January 30th, you may receive financial support or resources from a spouse, business partner, or collaborator. Be open to new ways of earning and managing money, and trust that the universe will provide for your needs and desires.

Review your budget and financial goals, and make sure that your spending aligns with your values and priorities. Consider investing in your personal and professional development, such as taking a course or hiring a coach, as this can pay off in the long run. Remember that true wealth comes from within, and that your inner state of abundance and gratitude is the foundation for your external reality.

Health:

In health, January 2025 is a month of deep healing, self-care, and inner transformation. With Mars, your traditional ruling planet, stationing retrograde in your 9th house of spirituality and higher learning, you may be called to explore alternative healing modalities or philosophies that support your well-being. Consider practices such as acupuncture, energy work, or shamanic journeying to help you release old patterns and traumas.

Take time to nurture your physical, emotional, and spiritual health through regular exercise, healthy eating, and stress management techniques. Make sure to get plenty of rest and sleep, and to create a daily routine that supports your overall well-being. Remember that true health comes from a holistic approach that addresses all aspects of your being.

Travel:

In travel, January 2025 may bring unexpected opportunities for adventure, learning, and personal growth. With Mars retrograde in your 9th house of travel and higher education, you may be called to revisit a place or culture that holds special meaning for you, or to explore new spiritual or philosophical traditions. Trust your intuition and be open to synchronicity and divine guidance.

If travel isn't possible or practical, find ways to bring a sense of adventure and exploration into your daily life. Take a class on a subject that fascinates you, attend a cultural event or festival, or connect with people from different backgrounds and perspectives. Remember that travel is not just about the destination, but about the journey of self-discovery and growth.

Insights from the Stars:

The celestial energies of January 2025 remind you of the power of surrender, trust, and inner transformation. With Mars retrograde in your 9th house of spirituality and higher learning, you are being called to let go of control, embrace the unknown, and allow yourself to be guided by a higher power or purpose. This is a time to face your fears, heal your wounds, and connect with your deepest truth and wisdom.

The Full Moon in Cancer on January 13th brings a powerful opportunity for emotional release, forgiveness, and new beginnings in your spiritual journey. Trust that the universe is supporting you every step of the way, and that your challenges and obstacles are ultimately serving your highest growth and evolution. Remember that you are a powerful creator and healer, and that your soul's purpose is to shine your light and love in the world.

Best Days of the Month:

- January 2nd: Vesta enters Scorpio - A powerful time to dedicate yourself to a higher purpose or cause.
- January 13th: Full Moon in Cancer - A culmination or turning point in your spiritual journey or educational pursuits.
- January 19th: Sun enters Aquarius - A fresh start in your home and family life, with opportunities for innovation and change.
- January 27th: Mercury enters Aquarius - Brilliant ideas and insights related to your home, family, or career.
- January 29th: New Moon in Aquarius - A powerful new beginning in your home and family life, with opportunities for growth and transformation.

February 2025

Overview Horoscope for the Month:

Scorpio, February 2025 is a month of deep emotional healing, spiritual awakening, and powerful new beginnings. As the shortest month of the year, it packs a punch with intense celestial energies that will catalyze your growth and transformation. Prepare to dive deep into your psyche, confront your shadows, and emerge as a more authentic and empowered version of yourself. Trust the process and know that you have the strength and resilience to handle whatever comes your way.

The month starts with a bang as Venus, the planet of love and relationships, enters fiery Aries on February 4th. This transit will bring a burst of passion, confidence, and assertiveness to your love life and creative pursuits. You may find yourself feeling more bold, spontaneous, and eager to take risks in matters of the heart. Use this energy to express your desires, pursue your dreams, and let your unique light shine.

On February 12th, the Full Moon in Leo illuminates your 10th house of career and public reputation. This powerful lunation will bring a culmination or turning point in your professional life, with opportunities for recognition, advancement, and success. Trust your talents and abilities, and don't be afraid to step into the spotlight and claim your rightful place. Remember that your work is a reflection of your soul's purpose and that you have the power to make a positive impact in the world.

Love:

In love, February 2025 is a month of passion, adventure, and new beginnings. With Venus entering Aries on February 4th, you'll be feeling more confident, assertive, and eager to take the lead in your relationships. If you're single, this is a fantastic time to put yourself out there, flirt with potential partners, and explore new romantic possibilities. Be bold, be playful, and let your unique personality shine.

If you're in a committed relationship, use this energy to spice things up and bring more excitement and spontaneity to your love life. Plan a surprise date, try a new hobby or activity together, or express your desires and fantasies with honesty and vulnerability. Remember that true intimacy requires both partners to be open, authentic, and willing to take risks.

On February 14th, Mercury enters dreamy Pisces, bringing a more romantic, intuitive, and imaginative energy to your communication style. Use this transit to express your feelings through poetry, music, or art, and to connect with your partner on a deeper, more soulful level. Trust your intuition and let your heart guide you towards more meaningful and fulfilling connections.

Career:

In your career, February 2025 is a month of powerful new beginnings, opportunities for growth, and public recognition. With the Full Moon in Leo on February 12th illuminating your 10th house of career and reputation, you may receive a promotion, award, or other forms of acknowledgement for your hard work and talents. Trust that your efforts are being seen and appreciated, and that you are making a positive impact in your field.

Take time to reflect on your long-term career goals and aspirations, and make sure that your work aligns with your values, passions, and purpose. If you're feeling unfulfilled or stuck in your current job, consider exploring new options or seeking out mentors who can support you in your professional development. Remember that your career is a journey, not a destination, and that every experience is an opportunity for growth and learning.

Finances:

In finances, February 2025 is a month of abundance, prosperity, and new opportunities for growth. With Jupiter, the planet of expansion and abundance, forming a sextile aspect to Chiron in your 5th house of creativity and self-expression, you may receive financial rewards or opportunities related to your artistic talents or entrepreneurial ventures. Trust your unique gifts and abilities, and don't be afraid to put yourself out there and showcase your work.

Review your budget and financial goals, and make sure that your spending aligns with your values and priorities. Consider investing in your personal and professional development, such as taking a course or attending a workshop, as this can pay off in the long run. Remember that true wealth comes from a sense of inner abundance, gratitude, and purpose, and that money is simply a tool to support your dreams and aspirations.

Health:

In health, February 2025 is a month of deep emotional healing, self-care, and inner transformation. With Mars, your traditional ruling planet, finally turning direct in Cancer on February 23rd, you may feel a renewed sense of energy, vitality, and motivation to take care of your physical and emotional well-being. Use this transit to establish healthy habits, routines, and boundaries that support your overall health and happiness.

Take time to nurture your body, mind, and soul through regular exercise, healthy eating, and stress-management techniques. Consider practices such as yoga, meditation, or therapy to help you release old patterns, traumas, and negative beliefs that may be holding you back. Remember that true health comes from a holistic approach that addresses all aspects of your being, and that self-love and self-care are essential for your growth and evolution.

Travel:

In travel, February 2025 may bring opportunities for spiritual pilgrimages, retreats, or journeys of self-discovery. With Neptune forming a conjunction with the True Node in Pisces on February 7th, you may feel called to visit sacred sites, connect with nature, or explore new spiritual practices and traditions. Trust your intuition and be open to synchronicity and divine guidance.

If travel isn't possible or practical, find ways to bring a sense of adventure, exploration, and wonder into your daily life. Take a nature walk, visit a local museum or art gallery, or attend a cultural event or workshop that expands your horizons and perspective. Remember that travel is not just about the destination, but about the journey of inner growth, learning, and transformation.

Insights from the Stars:

The celestial energies of February 2025 remind you of the power of vulnerability, authenticity, and emotional healing. With the Full Moon in Leo illuminating your 10th house of career and public reputation, you are being called to step into your true power and purpose, and to let your unique light shine in the world. Trust that your challenges, setbacks, and obstacles are ultimately serving your highest growth and evolution, and that you have the strength, resilience, and wisdom to overcome any adversity.

On February 27th, Saturn forms a semi-sextile aspect to Chiron in your 5th house of creativity, self-expression, and romance. This transit will bring opportunities for deep healing, self-acceptance, and transformation in these areas of your life. Trust that your wounds, insecurities, and vulnerabilities are actually your greatest teachers and sources of strength, and that by embracing them with love and compassion, you can unlock your true potential and purpose.

Best Days of the Month:

- February 4th: Venus enters Aries - A burst of passion, confidence, and assertiveness in your love life and creative pursuits.
- February 12th: Full Moon in Leo - A powerful culmination or turning point in

- your career, with opportunities for recognition and success.
- February 23rd: Mars turns direct in Cancer - A renewed sense of energy, vitality, and motivation to take care of your physical and emotional well-being.
- February 27th: New Moon in Pisces - A fresh start in your creative, romantic, and spiritual life, with opportunities for healing and transformation.
- February 28th: Mercury enters Aries - Bold, direct, and assertive communication in your relationships and professional life.

March 2025

Overview Horoscope for the Month:

Scorpio, March 2025 is a month of profound transformation, spiritual awakening, and powerful new beginnings. As the first month of spring, it brings a sense of renewal, rebirth, and growth that will catalyze your evolution and expansion. Prepare to shed old skin, release limiting patterns and beliefs, and embrace a new version of yourself that is more authentic, empowered, and aligned with your soul's purpose. Trust the journey and know that you are exactly where you need to be.

The month starts with a bang as Saturn, the planet of structure, responsibility, and karma, enters fiery Aries on March 24th. This major transit, which will last until May 2025, will bring a powerful new chapter in your life related to your work, health, and daily routines. You may feel called to take on more responsibility, discipline, and commitment in these areas, and to establish systems and structures that support your long-term goals and well-being. Embrace the challenge and know that your efforts will pay off in the long run.

On March 29th, the New Moon in Aries coincides with a powerful Partial Solar Eclipse, bringing a potent new beginning and fresh start in your 6th house of health, work, and service. This is a fantastic time to set intentions, launch new projects, or make positive changes in your lifestyle and habits. Trust your instincts and take bold action towards your goals, even if it means stepping outside your comfort zone. Remember that you have the strength, courage, and resilience to handle whatever comes your way.

Love:

In love, March 2025 is a month of deep emotional connections, spiritual intimacy, and powerful new beginnings. With Venus, the planet of love and relationships, traveling through sensitive Pisces for most of the month, you may find yourself craving a soul-level bond with your partner or seeking a relationship that transcends the physical realm. This is a time to open your heart, express your deepest feelings and desires, and create a safe space for love to flourish.

If you're in a committed relationship, take time to nurture your bond through shared activities that bring you closer together, such as a romantic getaway, couples' therapy, or spiritual practice. Be willing to be vulnerable and transparent about your fears, wounds, and dreams, and trust in the healing power of love and intimacy. Remember that true love requires both partners to show up fully and authentically.

If you're single, you may find yourself attracted to people who share your depth, intensity, and spiritual values. Look for partners who are willing to do the inner work of growth and transformation, and who appreciate your unique qualities and strengths. Trust your intuition and let your heart guide you towards meaningful connections. Remember that the most important relationship is the one you have with yourself.

Career:

In your career, March 2025 is a month of powerful new beginnings, opportunities for growth, and increased responsibility. With Saturn entering your 6th house of work and daily routines on March 24th, you may feel called to take on more leadership, discipline, and commitment in your job or business. This is a fantastic time to establish systems, structures, and routines that support your long-term goals and success. Trust your skills, talents, and experience, and don't be afraid to take on new challenges or responsibilities.

On March 29th, the New Moon in Aries and Partial Solar Eclipse in your 6th house of work and service brings a powerful fresh start and new beginning in your professional life. This is an excellent time to launch new projects, start a new job or business, or make positive changes in your work environment or habits. Trust your instincts and take bold action towards your goals, even if it means stepping outside your comfort zone. Remember that your work is a reflection of your soul's purpose and that you have the power to make a positive impact in the world.

Finances:

In finances, March 2025 is a month of new opportunities, increased discipline, and long-term planning. With Saturn entering your 6th house of work and daily routines on March 24th, you may feel called to take a more structured, responsible, and committed approach to your finances and resources. This is a fantastic time to create a budget, pay off debts, or start saving for the future. Trust that your efforts and discipline will pay off in the long run, and that you have the power to create financial stability and abundance.

On March 29th, the New Moon in Aries and Partial Solar Eclipse in your 6th house of work and service may bring unexpected financial opportunities or rewards related to your job or business. Be open to new ways of earning or managing money, and trust that the universe will provide for your needs and desires. Remember that true wealth comes from a sense of inner abundance, gratitude, and purpose, and that money is simply a tool to support your dreams and aspirations.

Health:

In health, March 2025 is a month of powerful new beginnings, increased discipline, and self-care. With Saturn entering your 6th house of health and well-being on March 24th, you may feel called to take a more structured, responsible, and committed approach to your physical, mental, and emotional health. This is a fantastic time to start a new exercise routine, healthy eating plan, or self-care practice that supports your long-term vitality and well-being. Trust that your efforts and discipline will pay off in the long run, and that you have the power to create a strong, healthy, and vibrant body, mind, and spirit.

On March 29th, the New Moon in Aries and Partial Solar Eclipse in your 6th house of health and well-being brings a powerful fresh start and new beginning in your self-care and wellness journey. This is an excellent time to make positive changes in your lifestyle, habits, and routines, and to prioritize your physical, mental, and emotional health. Trust your instincts and take bold action towards your wellness goals, even if it means stepping outside your comfort zone. Remember that true health comes from a holistic approach that addresses all aspects of your being, and that self-love and self-care are essential for your growth and evolution.

Travel:

In travel, March 2025 may bring unexpected opportunities for adventure, learning, and personal growth. With Neptune, the planet of spirituality and imagination, entering Aries on March 30th, you may feel called to explore new horizons, cultures, or spiritual practices that expand your perspective and awareness. Trust your intuition and be open to synchronicity and divine guidance.

If travel isn't possible or practical, find ways to bring a sense of adventure, exploration, and wonder into your daily life. Take a class on a subject that fascinates you, attend a cultural event or workshop, or connect with people from different backgrounds and walks of life. Remember that travel is not just about the destination, but about the journey of inner growth, learning, and transformation.

Insights from the Stars:

The celestial energies of March 2025 remind you of the power of discipline, commitment, and self-mastery. With Saturn entering your 6th house of work, health, and daily routines, you are being called to take responsibility for your life, to establish structures and systems that support your long-term goals and well-being, and to embrace the challenges and opportunities for growth and transformation. Trust that your efforts, discipline, and perseverance will pay off in the long run, and that you have the strength, resilience, and wisdom to overcome any obstacle or setback.

On March 29th, the New Moon in Aries and Partial Solar Eclipse in your 6th house of work, health, and service brings a powerful new beginning and fresh start in these areas of your life. Trust your instincts, take bold action towards your goals, and know that the universe is supporting you every step of the way. Remember that you are a powerful creator and manifestor, and that your thoughts, beliefs, and actions shape your reality. Embrace your inner warrior, leader, and healer, and know that you have the power to create a life of purpose, passion, and fulfillment.

Best Days of the Month:

- March 6th: Mars enters Leo - A burst of creativity, passion, and self-expression in your career and public life.
- March 14th: Full Moon in Virgo - A powerful culmination or turning point in your friendships, social networks, and community involvement.

- March 24th: Saturn enters Aries - A major new chapter and fresh start in your work, health, and daily routines.
- March 29th: New Moon in Aries and Partial Solar Eclipse - A potent new beginning and powerful fresh start in your work, health, and self-care journey.
- March 30th: Neptune enters Aries - A spiritual awakening and new beginning in your work, health, and daily routines, with opportunities for growth and transformation.

April 2025

Overview Horoscope for the Month:

Scorpio, April 2025 is a month of deep transformation, spiritual awakening, and powerful new beginnings. As the second month of spring, it brings a sense of renewal, growth, and expansion that will catalyze your evolution and self-discovery. Prepare to shed old patterns, beliefs, and limitations, and to embrace a new version of yourself that is more authentic, empowered, and aligned with your soul's purpose. Trust the journey and know that you are exactly where you need to be.

The month starts with a powerful astrological event as Saturn forms a sextile aspect to Uranus on April 4th. This rare and harmonious alignment between the planets of structure and innovation brings opportunities for positive change, progress, and breakthroughs in your life. You may feel a strong desire to break free from old routines, habits, or limitations, and to embrace new ways of living, working, and relating that are more authentic and fulfilling. Trust your intuition and be open to unexpected opportunities and synchronicities that align with your highest goals and aspirations.

On April 12th, the Full Moon in Libra illuminates your 12th house of spirituality, surrender, and inner growth. This powerful lunation brings a culmination or turning point in your spiritual journey, inviting you to release old patterns, wounds, or limitations that no longer serve your highest good. You may experience deep insights, revelations, or healing experiences that help you to let go of the past and embrace a new level of emotional freedom and inner peace. Trust the process of release and renewal, and know that you are supported by the universe every step of the way.

Love:

In love, April 2025 is a month of deep intimacy, emotional healing, and spiritual growth. With Venus, the planet of love and relationships, entering your opposite sign of Taurus on April 30th, you may feel a strong desire for stability, security, and commitment in your partnerships. This is a fantastic time to nurture your existing relationships with love, patience, and devotion, or to attract new connections that are grounded in shared values, mutual respect, and long-term compatibility. Trust your heart and be open to giving and receiving love in all its forms.

If you're in a committed relationship, take time to deepen your bond through shared activities that bring you closer together, such as a romantic getaway, couple's massage, or nature retreat. Be willing to communicate your needs, desires, and boundaries with honesty and vulnerability, and to listen to your partner with an open heart and mind. Remember that true intimacy requires both partners to show up fully and authentically, and to support each other's growth and evolution.

If you're single, you may attract people who share your values, interests, and spiritual path. Look for partners who are grounded, reliable, and committed to personal growth and self-discovery. Trust your intuition and take your time getting to know potential partners before jumping into a serious relationship. Remember that the most important relationship is the one you have with yourself, and that self-love and self-care are essential for attracting healthy, fulfilling connections.

Career:

In your career, April 2025 is a month of positive change, progress, and innovation. With Saturn forming a sextile aspect to Uranus on April 4th, you may experience unexpected opportunities, breakthroughs, or advancements in your work or business. This is a fantastic time to take risks, embrace new challenges, and think outside the box in your professional life. Trust your skills, talents, and unique perspective, and don't be afraid to stand out from the crowd or take a leadership role in your field.

On April 16th, Mercury enters Aries, bringing a burst of energy, confidence, and assertiveness to your communication and networking skills. Use this transit to pitch your ideas, promote your work, or connect with influential people in your industry. Remember that your voice and message have the power to inspire, motivate, and create positive change in the world.

Finances:

In finances, April 2025 is a month of abundance, prosperity, and positive change. With Jupiter, the planet of expansion and abundance, forming a sextile aspect to Chiron in your 6th house of work and service on April 18th, you may experience financial rewards, opportunities, or breakthroughs related to your job, business, or investments. Trust that your efforts, skills, and talents are being recognized and valued, and that the universe is conspiring to support your financial growth and success.

On April 21st, Saturn forms a conjunction with the True Node in your 5th house of creativity, self-expression, and joy. This powerful alignment invites you to align your financial goals and strategies with your authentic passions, talents, and purpose. You may feel called to invest in your creative projects, start a side hustle, or pursue a career that allows you to express your unique gifts and abilities. Trust that when you follow your heart and do what you love, abundance and prosperity will naturally flow into your life.

Health:

In health, April 2025 is a month of deep healing, self-care, and spiritual growth. With Mars, your traditional ruling planet, entering Leo on April 18th, you may feel a renewed sense of vitality, confidence, and motivation to take care of your physical, mental, and emotional well-being. Use this transit to establish healthy habits, routines, and practices that support your long-term health and happiness, such as regular exercise, nutritious eating, and stress-management techniques.

On April 12th, the Full Moon in Libra illuminates your 12th house of spirituality, surrender, and inner growth, inviting you to release old patterns, traumas, or limitations that may be affecting your health and well-being. You may experience deep insights, revelations, or healing experiences that help you to let go of the past and embrace a new level of emotional freedom and inner peace. Trust the process of release and renewal, and know that you are supported by the universe every step of the way.

Travel:

In travel, April 2025 may bring opportunities for spiritual pilgrimages, retreats, or journeys of self-discovery. With Venus entering Taurus on April 30th, you may feel called to visit beautiful, natural settings that allow you to reconnect with your senses, your body, and the earth. Consider taking a trip to a peaceful, serene location such as a mountain retreat, beach resort, or eco-lodge, where you can unplug from technology, slow down, and immerse yourself in the healing energy of nature.

If travel isn't possible or practical, find ways to bring a sense of beauty, pleasure, and relaxation into your daily life. Take a scenic drive, visit a local park or garden, or create a cozy, inviting space in your home that allows you to unwind and recharge. Remember that travel is not just about the destination, but about the journey of inner growth, self-discovery, and connection with the world around you.

Insights from the Stars:

The celestial energies of April 2025 remind you of the power of surrender, faith, and inner growth. With the Full Moon in Libra illuminating your 12th house of spirituality and surrender on April 12th, you are being called to let go of control, trust in the flow of life, and allow yourself to be guided by a higher power or purpose. This is a time to face your fears, heal your wounds, and connect with your deepest truth and wisdom.

On April 17th, Jupiter forms a sesquadrate aspect to Pluto in your 3rd house of communication and learning. This challenging alignment may bring up intense power struggles, conflicts, or confrontations in your relationships or interactions with others. You may need to stand up for your beliefs, values, or boundaries, or to speak truth to power in some way. Trust your intuition and inner strength, and know that your voice and message have the power to create positive change and transformation in the world.

Best Days of the Month:

- April 4th: Saturn sextile Uranus - Positive change, progress, and innovation in your career, finances, and personal growth.
- April 12th: Full Moon in Libra - A powerful culmination or turning point in your spiritual journey, with opportunities for deep healing, release, and renewal.
- April 16th: Mercury enters Aries - A burst of energy, confidence, and assertiveness in your communication and networking skills.
- April 18th: Jupiter sextile Chiron - Financial rewards, opportunities, or

breakthroughs related to your job, business, or investments.
- April 30th: Venus enters Taurus - A desire for stability, security, and commitment in your relationships, with opportunities for deep intimacy, emotional healing, and spiritual growth.

May 2025

Overview Horoscope for the Month:

Scorpio, May 2025 is a month of intense transformation, spiritual growth, and personal empowerment. As the final month of spring, it brings a sense of culmination, completion, and new beginnings that will catalyze your evolution and self-discovery. Prepare to shed old patterns, beliefs, and limitations that no longer serve your highest good, and to embrace a new level of authenticity, freedom, and alignment with your soul's purpose. Trust the journey and know that you are exactly where you need to be.

The month starts with a powerful astrological event as Saturn semi-squares Pluto on May 1st. This challenging alignment between the planets of structure and transformation may bring up intense power struggles, conflicts, or confrontations in your relationships, career, or personal life. You may need to confront deep-seated fears, shadows, or limitations that are holding you back from your full potential, or to make difficult choices and changes that align with your true values and desires. Trust your inner strength and resilience, and know that the challenges you face are ultimately serving your highest growth and evolution.

On May 12th, the Full Moon in Scorpio illuminates your 1st house of self, identity, and personal power. This powerful lunation brings a culmination or turning point in your journey of self-discovery and transformation, inviting you to claim your authentic truth, voice, and purpose in the world. You may experience deep insights, revelations, or breakthroughs that help you to let go of old patterns of self-doubt, fear, or limitation, and to embrace a new level of confidence, courage, and self-expression. Trust the process of rebirth and renewal, and know that you have the power to create a life that truly reflects your deepest passions, values, and desires.

Love:

In love, May 2025 is a month of deep intimacy, emotional healing, and spiritual growth. With Venus, the planet of love and relationships, entering your 8th house of deep bonding and transformation on May 11th, you may feel a strong desire for soul-level connections, vulnerability, and emotional intensity in your partnerships. This is a fantastic time to deepen your existing relationships with honesty, trust, and mutual support, or to attract new connections that are based on shared values, passions, and spiritual growth. Trust your heart and be open to giving and receiving love in all its forms, even if it means facing your fears or shadows in the process.

If you're in a committed relationship, take time to explore the deeper layers of your connection through intimate conversations, shared adventures, or spiritual practices. Be willing to be vulnerable and transparent about your fears, desires, and dreams, and to support your partner's growth and evolution with love, compassion, and understanding. Remember that true intimacy requires both partners to show up fully and authentically, and to create a safe space for emotional healing and transformation.

If you're single, you may attract people who share your depth, intensity, and spiritual values. Look for partners who are willing to do the inner work of growth and self-discovery, and who appreciate your unique gifts and strengths. Trust your intuition and take your time getting to know potential partners before jumping into a serious relationship. Remember that the most important relationship is the one you have with yourself, and that self-love and self-care are essential for attracting healthy, fulfilling connections.

Career:
In your career, May 2025 is a month of power, success, and personal achievement. With Jupiter, the planet of expansion and abundance, forming a

biquintile aspect to Pluto in your 3rd house of communication and networking on May 30th, you may experience unexpected opportunities, breakthroughs, or recognition in your work or business. This is a fantastic time to showcase your unique talents, ideas, and leadership skills, and to take bold action towards your professional goals and aspirations. Trust that your efforts and dedication are being seen and valued, and that the universe is conspiring to support your success and fulfillment.

On May 18th, Jupiter forms a square aspect to the True Node in your 6th house of work, health, and service. This challenging alignment may bring up questions or doubts about your current path or purpose, or highlight areas where you need to make changes or adjustments to align with your true calling. Trust your inner guidance and be open to new opportunities or directions that feel authentic and meaningful to you. Remember that your work is a reflection of your soul's purpose, and that you have the power to create a career that truly reflects your passions, values, and unique gifts.

Finances:

In finances, May 2025 is a month of abundance, prosperity, and positive change. With Jupiter, the planet of expansion and abundance, forming a sextile aspect to Chiron in your 6th house of work and service on May 18th, you may experience financial rewards, opportunities, or breakthroughs related to your job, business, or investments. Trust that your efforts, skills, and talents are being recognized and valued, and that the universe is supporting your financial growth and success.

On May 24th, Saturn enters your 6th house of work, health, and daily routines, bringing a new level of structure, discipline, and responsibility to your financial life. This is a fantastic time to create a budget, set financial goals, and develop a long-term plan for wealth and abundance. You may need to make some sacrifices or adjustments in the short term, but trust that your efforts will pay off in the long run. Remember that true prosperity comes from aligning your finances with your values, purpose, and highest good.

Health:

In health, May 2025 is a month of deep healing, self-care, and spiritual growth. With the Full Moon in your sign on May 12th, you may experience a powerful release or breakthrough in your physical, emotional, or spiritual well-being. This is a fantastic time to let go of old patterns, habits, or beliefs that are no longer serving your highest good, and to embrace a new level of vitality, energy, and self-love. Trust the process of renewal and regeneration, and know that you have the power to create a healthy, vibrant, and fulfilling life.

On May 24th, Saturn enters your 6th house of health and daily routines, bringing a new level of structure, discipline, and commitment to your self-care practices. This is a fantastic time to establish healthy habits, routines, and rituals that support your long-term well-being, such as regular exercise, nutritious eating, and stress-management techniques. You may need to make some sacrifices or adjustments in the short term, but trust that your efforts will pay off in the long run. Remember that true health comes from aligning your mind, body, and spirit with your highest good and purpose.

Travel:

In travel, May 2025 may bring opportunities for deep transformation, spiritual growth, and personal empowerment. With Venus entering your 8th house of deep bonding and transformation on May 11th, you may feel called to explore hidden or mystical places that allow you to connect with your inner world and the mysteries of life. Consider taking a trip to a sacred site, ancient ruins, or a place of natural wonder, where you can immerse yourself in the energy of transformation and rebirth.

If travel isn't possible or practical, find ways to bring a sense of depth, intensity, and spiritual growth into your daily life. Explore your inner world through practices such as meditation, journaling, or dream work, or seek out experiences that challenge you to step outside your comfort zone and embrace new perspectives. Remember that travel is not just about the destination, but about the journey of self-discovery and transformation.

Insights from the Stars:

The celestial energies of May 2025 remind you of the power of surrender, trust, and inner transformation. With the Full Moon in your sign on May 12th, you are being called to let go of control, embrace the unknown, and allow yourself to be guided by your deepest truth and wisdom. This is a time to face your fears, heal your wounds, and connect with your authentic self and purpose.

On May 18th, Jupiter forms a square aspect to the True Node in your 6th house of work, health, and service. This challenging alignment may bring up questions or doubts about your current path or purpose, or highlight areas where you need to make changes or adjustments to align with your true calling. Trust your inner guidance and be open to new opportunities or directions that feel authentic and meaningful to you. Remember that your work is a reflection of your soul's purpose, and that you have the power to create a life that truly reflects your passions, values, and unique gifts.

Best Days of the Month:

- May 1st: Saturn semi-square Pluto - Intense power struggles, conflicts, or confrontations that ultimately serve your highest growth and evolution.
- May 12th: Full Moon in Scorpio - A powerful culmination or turning point in your journey of self-discovery and transformation.
- May 18th: Jupiter sextile Chiron - Financial rewards, opportunities, or breakthroughs related to your job, business, or investments.
- May 24th: Saturn enters 6th house - A new level of structure, discipline, and commitment to your work, health, and daily routines.
- May 30th: Jupiter biquintile Pluto - Unexpected opportunities, breakthroughs, or recognition in your career or business.

June 2025

Overview Horoscope for the Month:

Scorpio, June 2025 is a month of deep introspection, emotional healing, and spiritual growth. As the first month of summer, it brings a sense of warmth, vitality, and inner illumination that will catalyze your evolution and self-discovery. Prepare to dive deep into your psyche, confront your shadows and fears, and emerge with a renewed sense of purpose, power, and alignment with your soul's path. Trust the journey and know that you are exactly where you need to be.

The month starts with a powerful astrological event as Jupiter, the planet of expansion and growth, squares Saturn, your traditional ruler, on June 15th. This challenging alignment between the planets of opportunity and restriction may bring up tensions or obstacles in your personal or professional life, particularly around issues of freedom, responsibility, and long-term goals. You may need to find a balance between your desire for growth and adventure, and your need for structure, discipline, and stability. Trust your inner wisdom and be open to making necessary adjustments or compromises that align with your highest good.

On June 25th, the New Moon in Cancer illuminates your 9th house of higher learning, travel, and spiritual growth. This powerful lunation brings a new beginning or fresh start in your journey of knowledge, wisdom, and self-discovery. You may feel called to expand your horizons, explore new cultures or philosophies, or deepen your spiritual practice. Trust your intuition and be open to new opportunities or experiences that broaden your perspective and enrich your understanding of yourself and the world.

Love:

In love, June 2025 is a month of emotional intimacy, vulnerability, and spiritual connection. With Venus, the planet of love and relationships, entering your 9th house of higher learning and spiritual growth on June 4th, you may feel a strong desire for a partnership that expands your mind, heart, and soul. This is a fantastic time to connect with someone who shares your values, beliefs, and thirst for knowledge, or to deepen your existing relationship through shared learning, travel, or spiritual practices. Trust your heart and be open to giving and receiving love in all its forms, even if it means stepping outside your comfort zone.

If you're in a committed relationship, take time to explore new ways of connecting and communicating with your partner, such as learning a new language together, taking a class or workshop, or embarking on a spiritual retreat. Be willing to be vulnerable and transparent about your hopes, fears, and dreams, and to support your partner's growth and evolution with love, compassion, and understanding. Remember that true intimacy requires both partners to show up fully and authentically, and to create a safe space for emotional and spiritual growth.

If you're single, you may attract people who share your intellectual curiosity, adventurous spirit, and spiritual values. Look for partners who inspire you to learn, grow, and expand your horizons, and who appreciate your unique gifts and strengths. Trust your intuition and take your time getting to know potential partners before jumping into a serious relationship. Remember that the most important relationship is the one you have with yourself, and that self-love and self-discovery are essential for attracting healthy, fulfilling connections.

Career:

In your career, June 2025 is a month of growth, learning, and new opportunities. With Mars, your traditional ruler, entering your 10th house of career and public reputation on June 17th, you may feel a strong drive to advance your professional goals, take on new challenges, and make your mark in the world. This is a fantastic time to assert your leadership skills, showcase your talents and expertise, and pursue opportunities that align with your passions and purpose. Trust that your efforts and dedication are being seen and valued, and that the universe is supporting your success and fulfillment.

On June 18th, Jupiter forms a quincunx aspect to Pluto in your 3rd house of communication and networking. This challenging alignment may bring up power struggles or conflicts in your professional relationships or interactions, particularly around issues of control, influence, or authority. You may need to navigate complex dynamics or negotiations with tact, diplomacy, and a clear sense of your own boundaries and values. Trust your inner strength and integrity, and be open to finding creative solutions or compromises that serve the highest good of all involved.

Finances:

In finances, June 2025 is a month of abundance, prosperity, and positive change. With Jupiter, the planet of expansion and abundance, entering your 10th house of career and public reputation on June 9th, you may experience financial rewards, opportunities, or breakthroughs related to your job, business, or investments. Trust that your efforts, skills, and talents are being recognized and valued, and that the universe is supporting your financial growth and success.

On June 15th, Jupiter squares Saturn in your 5th house of creativity, self-expression, and joy. This challenging alignment may bring up tensions or obstacles around your ability to manifest abundance through your unique gifts and talents, or to find a balance between work and play, responsibility and pleasure. You may need to make some sacrifices or adjustments in the short term, but trust that your efforts will pay off in the long run. Remember that true prosperity comes from aligning your finances with your values, purpose, and highest good.

Health:

In health, June 2025 is a month of vitality, energy, and inner growth. With the Sun, the planet of life force and vitality, entering your 9th house of higher learning and spiritual growth on June 20th, you may feel a renewed sense of purpose, passion, and inner illumination. This is a fantastic time to expand your knowledge and understanding of health and wellness, explore new healing modalities or practices, and connect with your inner wisdom and guidance. Trust that your body, mind, and spirit are always working towards balance, harmony, and wholeness.

On June 25th, the New Moon in Cancer falls in your 9th house, bringing a new beginning or fresh start in your journey of health and well-being. This is a fantastic time to set intentions around your physical, emotional, and spiritual health, and to take action towards your goals and desires. You may feel called to start a new exercise routine, change your diet or lifestyle, or explore alternative therapies or practices that support your overall vitality and resilience. Trust the process of growth and transformation, and know that you have the power to create a healthy, vibrant, and fulfilling life.

Travel:

In travel, June 2025 may bring opportunities for adventure, learning, and personal growth. With Venus entering your 9th house of travel and higher learning on June 4th, you may feel called to explore new cultures, landscapes, or experiences that expand your mind, heart, and soul. Consider taking a trip to a foreign country, enrolling in a study abroad program, or embarking on a spiritual pilgrimage that allows you to connect with your inner truth and wisdom.

If travel isn't possible or practical, find ways to bring a sense of adventure, curiosity, and growth into your daily life. Explore your local community or region with fresh eyes, attend cultural events or festivals, or connect with people from different backgrounds and perspectives. Remember that travel is not just about the destination, but about the journey of self-discovery and transformation.

Insights from the Stars:

The celestial energies of June 2025 remind you of the power of growth, learning, and inner illumination. With Jupiter entering your 10th house of career and public reputation on June 9th, you are being called to expand your vision, take risks, and pursue opportunities that align with your highest purpose and potential. This is a time to trust your inner guidance, embrace your unique gifts and talents, and shine your light in the world.

On June 18th, Jupiter forms a quincunx aspect to Pluto in your 3rd house of communication and networking. This challenging alignment may bring up power struggles or conflicts in your relationships or interactions, particularly around issues of control, influence, or authority. Trust your inner strength and integrity, and be open to finding creative solutions or compromises that serve the highest good of all involved. Remember that your words and ideas have the power to transform and heal, and that you are a catalyst for positive change in the world.

Best Days of the Month:

- June 4th: Venus enters 9th house - A desire for a partnership that expands your mind, heart, and soul, and opportunities for travel, learning, and spiritual growth.
- June 9th: Jupiter enters 10th house - Financial rewards, opportunities, or breakthroughs related to your career or public reputation.
- June 17th: Mars enters 10th house - A strong drive to advance your professional goals, take on new challenges, and make your mark in the world.
- June 20th: Sun enters 9th house - A renewed sense of purpose, passion, and inner illumination, and opportunities for growth and self-discovery.
- June 25th: New Moon in Cancer - A new beginning or fresh start in your journey of higher learning, travel, and spiritual growth, and intentions for health and well-being.

July 2025

Overview Horoscope for the Month:

Scorpio, July 2025 is a month of emotional intensity, spiritual awakening, and personal transformation. As the peak of summer, it brings a sense of heat, passion, and inner fire that will catalyze your evolution and self-discovery. Prepare to face your deepest fears, desires, and shadows, and to emerge with a renewed sense of power, purpose, and alignment with your soul's path. Trust the journey and know that you are exactly where you need to be.

The month starts with a powerful astrological event as Uranus, the planet of sudden change and awakening, turns retrograde in your 7th house of partnerships on July 6th. This transit may bring unexpected shifts, challenges, or breakthroughs in your closest relationships, particularly around issues of freedom, individuality, and authenticity. You may need to confront patterns of codependency, power struggles, or limiting beliefs that are holding you back from true intimacy and connection. Trust your inner wisdom and be open to making necessary changes or adjustments that align with your highest good.

On July 10th, the Full Moon in Capricorn illuminates your 3rd house of communication, learning, and self-expression. This powerful lunation brings a culmination or turning point in your journey of knowledge, understanding, and mental growth. You may receive important news, insights, or realizations that shift your perspective and understanding of yourself and the world. Trust your intuition and be open to new ideas, conversations, or experiences that expand your mind and enrich your sense of purpose and meaning.

Love:

In love, July 2025 is a month of deep intimacy, emotional healing, and spiritual connection. With Venus, the planet of love and relationships, entering your 10th house of career and public reputation on July 30th, you may feel a strong desire for a partnership that supports your professional goals, ambitions, and sense of purpose. This is a fantastic time to connect with someone who shares your values, work ethic, and vision for the future, or to deepen your existing relationship through shared projects, goals, or public appearances. Trust your heart and be open to giving and receiving love in all its forms, even if it means stepping into the spotlight or taking on new responsibilities.

If you're in a committed relationship, take time to explore new ways of supporting and empowering each other, such as collaborating on a business venture, attending networking events together, or taking on a leadership role in your community. Be willing to be vulnerable and transparent about your hopes, fears, and dreams, and to support your partner's growth and success with love, encouragement, and practical assistance. Remember that true partnership requires both individuals to show up fully and authentically, and to create a safe space for emotional and practical support.

If you're single, you may attract people who share your ambition, drive, and sense of purpose. Look for partners who inspire you to reach for your goals, take risks, and make a positive impact in the world, and who appreciate your unique gifts and strengths. Trust your intuition and take your time getting to know potential partners before jumping into a serious relationship. Remember that the most important relationship is the one you have with yourself, and that self-love and self-respect are essential for attracting healthy, fulfilling connections.

Career:

In your career, July 2025 is a month of growth, success, and public recognition. With the Sun, the planet of vitality and self-expression, entering your 10th house of career and public reputation on July 22nd, you may feel a strong drive to advance your professional goals, take on new challenges, and make your mark in the world. This is a fantastic time to showcase your talents, expertise, and leadership skills, and to pursue opportunities that align with your passions and purpose. Trust that your efforts and dedication are being seen and valued, and that the universe is supporting your success and fulfillment.

On July 18th, Jupiter forms a square aspect to Chiron in your 6th house of work, health, and service. This challenging alignment may bring up wounds, insecurities, or limitations around your ability to manifest your true calling or to find a sense of meaning and purpose in your daily work. You may need to confront patterns of self-doubt, perfectionism, or people-pleasing that are holding you back from authentic self-expression and fulfillment. Trust your inner healing process and be open to finding creative solutions or adjustments that allow you to align your work with your highest values and aspirations.

Finances:

In finances, July 2025 is a month of abundance, prosperity, and positive change. With Venus, the planet of love and money, entering your 10th house of career and public reputation on July 30th, you may experience financial rewards, opportunities, or breakthroughs related to your professional achievements, status, or public image. Trust that your efforts, skills, and talents are being recognized and valued, and that the universe is supporting your financial growth and success.

On July 13th, Saturn, your traditional ruler, turns retrograde in your 5th house of creativity, self-expression, and joy. This transit may bring up challenges or limitations around your ability to manifest abundance through your unique gifts and talents, or to find a sense of play, pleasure, and fulfillment in your financial life. You may need to confront patterns of scarcity, self-doubt, or over-responsibility that are holding you back from true prosperity and joy. Trust your inner wisdom and be open to making necessary adjustments or sacrifices that align with your highest values and long-term goals.

Health:

In health, July 2025 is a month of deep healing, transformation, and inner growth. With Mars, the planet of energy and action, entering your 12th house of spirituality, surrender, and inner work on June 22nd, you may feel a strong drive to explore your inner world, confront your shadows and fears, and release old patterns and traumas that are holding you back from true health and wholeness. This is a fantastic time to engage in practices such as meditation, therapy, or energy healing that support your emotional, mental, and spiritual well-being.

On July 10th, the Full Moon in Capricorn falls in your 3rd house of communication, learning, and self-expression, bringing a culmination or turning point in your journey of self-discovery and mental growth. You may receive important insights, realizations, or messages that shift your perspective and understanding of your health and well-being. Trust your intuition and be open to new ideas, practices, or modalities that support your overall vitality and resilience. Remember that true health comes from a holistic approach that addresses all aspects of your being - physical, emotional, mental, and spiritual.

Travel:

In travel, July 2025 may bring opportunities for personal growth, self-discovery, and inner exploration. With Mars entering your 12th house of spirituality and inner work on June 22nd, you may feel called to embark on a journey of self-reflection, emotional healing, or spiritual awakening. Consider taking a solo retreat, attending a meditation or yoga workshop, or visiting a sacred site or natural wonder that allows you to connect with your inner wisdom and guidance.

If travel isn't possible or practical, find ways to bring a sense of inner exploration, self-discovery, and healing into your daily life. Engage in practices such as journaling, dream work, or creative expression that allow you to access your subconscious mind and inner world. Remember that travel is not just about the destination, but about the journey of self-discovery and transformation.

Insights from the Stars:

The celestial energies of July 2025 remind you of the power of emotional healing, spiritual awakening, and inner transformation. With Uranus turning retrograde in your 7th house of partnerships on July 6th, you are being called to confront patterns of codependency, power struggles, or limiting beliefs that are holding you back from true intimacy and connection. This is a time to trust your inner wisdom, embrace your individuality and authenticity, and make necessary changes or adjustments that align with your highest good.

On July 18th, Jupiter forms a square aspect to Chiron in your 6th house of work, health, and service. This challenging alignment may bring up wounds, insecurities, or limitations around your ability to manifest your true calling or to find a sense of meaning and purpose in your daily work. Trust your inner healing process and be open to finding creative solutions or adjustments that allow you to align your work with your highest values and aspirations. Remember that your challenges and struggles are ultimately serving your growth and evolution, and that you have the power to transform your pain into purpose and passion.

Best Days of the Month:

- July 6th: Uranus turns retrograde in 7th house - Unexpected shifts, challenges, or breakthroughs in your closest relationships that serve your growth and awakening.
- July 10th: Full Moon in Capricorn - A culmination or turning point in your journey of communication, learning, and self-expression, and insights for health and well-being.
- July 22nd: Sun enters 10th house - A strong drive to advance your professional goals, take on new challenges, and make your mark in the world.
- July 30th: Venus enters 10th house - Financial rewards, opportunities, or breakthroughs related to your career or public reputation, and a desire for a

partnership that supports your professional goals and ambitions.
- July 31st: Mercury enters 10th house - Clear communication, networking, and mental focus in your career and public life.

August 2025

Overview Horoscope for the Month:

Scorpio, August 2025 is a month of deep transformation, emotional healing, and spiritual growth. As the final month of summer, it brings a sense of culmination, completion, and new beginnings that will catalyze your evolution and self-discovery. Prepare to shed old patterns, beliefs, and limitations that no longer serve your highest good, and to embrace a new level of authenticity, freedom, and alignment with your soul's purpose. Trust the journey and know that you have the strength and resilience to handle whatever comes your way.

The month starts with a powerful astrological event as Saturn, your traditional ruler, forms a sextile aspect to Uranus on August 11th. This harmonious alignment between the planets of structure and innovation brings opportunities for positive change, progress, and breakthroughs in your personal and professional life. You may feel a strong desire to break free from old routines, habits, or limitations, and to embrace new ways of living, working, and relating that are more authentic and fulfilling. Trust your intuition and be open to unexpected opportunities and synchronicities that align with your highest goals and aspirations.

On August 9th, the Full Moon in Aquarius illuminates your 4th house of home, family, and emotional foundations. This powerful lunation brings a culmination or turning point in your journey of emotional healing, self-care, and inner growth. You may experience deep insights, revelations, or breakthroughs that help you to release old wounds, patterns, or family dynamics that are holding you back from true happiness and fulfillment. Trust the process of release and renewal, and know that you have the power to create a nurturing, supportive, and loving environment for yourself and your loved ones.

Love:

In love, August 2025 is a month of deep intimacy, emotional healing, and spiritual growth. With Venus, the planet of love and relationships, entering your 11th house of friendships and social connections on August 25th, you may feel a strong desire for partnerships that are based on shared values, ideals, and visions for the future. This is a fantastic time to connect with like-minded individuals who share your passions, interests, and goals, or to deepen your existing relationships through group activities, social events, or humanitarian causes. Trust your heart and be open to giving and receiving love in all its forms, even if it means stepping outside your comfort zone or taking risks.

If you're in a committed relationship, take time to explore new ways of connecting and communicating with your partner, such as joining a club or organization together, attending workshops or seminars, or volunteering for a cause that you both care about. Be willing to be vulnerable and transparent about your hopes, dreams, and ideals, and to support your partner's growth and evolution with love, encouragement, and understanding. Remember that true intimacy requires both partners to show up fully and authentically, and to create a safe space for emotional and spiritual growth.

If you're single, you may attract people who share your values, interests, and vision for the future. Look for partners who inspire you to be your best self, who challenge you to grow and evolve, and who appreciate your unique gifts and strengths. Trust your intuition and take your time getting to know potential partners before jumping into a serious relationship. Remember that the most important relationship is the one you have with yourself, and that self-love and self-acceptance are essential for attracting healthy, fulfilling connections.

Career:

In your career, August 2025 is a month of innovation, progress, and positive change. With Uranus, the planet of sudden change and innovation, forming a sextile aspect to Saturn on August 11th, you may experience unexpected opportunities, breakthroughs, or advancements in your work or business. This is a fantastic time to take risks, embrace new challenges, and think outside the box in your professional life. Trust your unique talents, skills, and perspective, and don't be afraid to stand out from the crowd or take a leadership role in your field.

On August 6th, Mars, your traditional ruler, enters your 12th house of spirituality, surrender, and inner growth. This transit may bring a period of introspection, reflection, and inner work in your professional life. You may feel called to explore your deeper purpose, values, and motivations, and to make sure that your work aligns with your spiritual path and highest good. Trust your intuition and be open to making necessary changes or adjustments that allow you to express your authentic self and make a positive impact in the world.

Finances:

In finances, August 2025 is a month of abundance, prosperity, and positive change. With Jupiter, the planet of expansion and abundance, forming a trine aspect to the True Node in your 6th house of work and service on September 3rd, you may experience financial rewards, opportunities, or breakthroughs related to your job, business, or investments. Trust that your efforts, skills, and talents are being recognized and valued, and that the universe is supporting your financial growth and success.

On August 11th, Ceres, the asteroid of nurturing and abundance, turns retrograde in your 6th house of work and health. This transit may bring a period of reflection and re-evaluation around your ability to manifest abundance through your daily work and routines, or to find a sense of purpose and fulfillment in your financial life. You may need to confront patterns of scarcity, self-doubt, or over-giving that are holding you back from true prosperity and self-care. Trust your inner wisdom and be open to making necessary adjustments or boundaries that align with your highest values and long-term goals.

Health:

In health, August 2025 is a month of deep healing, self-care, and inner transformation. With the Full Moon in Aquarius on August 9th illuminating your 4th house of home, family, and emotional foundations, you may experience a powerful release or breakthrough in your physical, emotional, or spiritual well-being. This is a fantastic time to let go of old patterns, habits, or beliefs that are no longer serving your highest good, and to embrace a new level of self-love, self-care, and inner peace. Trust the process of renewal and regeneration, and know that you have the power to create a healthy, vibrant, and fulfilling life.

On August 6th, Mars enters your 12th house of spirituality, surrender, and inner growth, bringing a period of introspection, reflection, and inner work in your health and well-being. You may feel called to explore alternative healing modalities, spiritual practices, or self-care routines that support your physical, emotional, and spiritual health. Trust your intuition and be open to making necessary changes or adjustments that allow you to align your mind, body, and spirit with your highest good and purpose.

Travel:

In travel, August 2025 may bring opportunities for social connections, group activities, and humanitarian causes. With Venus entering your 11th house of friendships and social networks on August 25th, you may feel called to travel with friends, join a club or organization, or participate in a service project or volunteer opportunity. Consider taking a trip with like-minded individuals who share your passions, interests, and vision for the future, or exploring new cultures and communities that align with your values and ideals.

If travel isn't possible or practical, find ways to bring a sense of connection, purpose, and social engagement into your daily life. Attend local events, workshops, or gatherings that allow you to meet new people, learn new skills, or make a positive impact in your community. Remember that travel is not just about the destination, but about the journey of self-discovery, growth, and connection with others.

Insights from the Stars:

The celestial energies of August 2025 remind you of the power of authenticity, innovation, and positive change. With Saturn forming a sextile aspect to Uranus on August 11th, you are being called to break free from old patterns, limitations, and structures that are holding you back from your true potential and purpose. This is a time to embrace your unique talents, perspective, and vision, and to trust that the universe is supporting your growth and evolution.

On August 28th, Uranus, the planet of sudden change and awakening, forms a sextile aspect to Neptune in your 5th house of creativity, self-expression, and joy. This harmonious alignment brings opportunities for spiritual growth, artistic inspiration, and unconditional love in your life. You may feel a strong desire to express your authentic self, explore your imagination and intuition, or connect with a higher power or purpose. Trust your inner guidance and be open to unexpected insights, synchronicities, or encounters that align with your highest good and soul's path.

Best Days of the Month:

- August 9th: Full Moon in Aquarius - A powerful culmination or turning point in your journey of emotional healing, self-care, and inner growth.
- August 11th: Saturn sextile Uranus - Positive change, progress, and breakthroughs in your personal and professional life, with opportunities for authenticity and innovation.
- August 12th: Mercury turns direct - Clear communication, mental focus, and forward momentum in your career, public image, and long-term goals.
- August 25th: Venus enters 11th house - Opportunities for social connections, group activities, and humanitarian causes, with a desire for partnerships based on shared values and visions.
- August 28th: Uranus sextile Neptune - Spiritual growth, artistic inspiration, and unconditional love in your life, with

opportunities for authentic self-expression and higher purpose.

September 2025

Overview Horoscope for the Month:

Scorpio, September 2025 is a month of profound transformation, spiritual awakening, and personal empowerment. As the first month of autumn, it brings a sense of change, letting go, and new beginnings that will catalyze your evolution and self-discovery. Prepare to shed old patterns, beliefs, and limitations that no longer serve your highest good, and to embrace a new level of authenticity, wisdom, and alignment with your soul's purpose. Trust the journey and know that you have the strength and resilience to handle whatever comes your way.

The month starts with a powerful astrological event as Mars, your traditional ruler, enters your sign on September 22nd. This transit, which lasts until November 4th, will bring a surge of energy, passion, and motivation to pursue your goals, assert your needs and desires, and make your mark on the world. You may feel more confident, courageous, and ready to take bold action towards your dreams and aspirations. Use this time to focus on your personal growth, self-discovery, and self-empowerment, and to let go of any fears, doubts, or limitations that have been holding you back.

On September 7th, the Full Moon in Pisces illuminates your 5th house of creativity, self-expression, and joy. This powerful lunation, which coincides with a Total Lunar Eclipse, brings a culmination or turning point in your journey of artistic pursuits, romantic relationships, and personal fulfillment. You may experience deep emotions, revelations, or breakthroughs that help you to release old patterns, wounds, or blocks that have been preventing you from fully expressing your authentic self and enjoying life to the fullest. Trust the process of release and renewal, and know that you have the power to create a life filled with love, passion, and purpose.

Love:

In love, September 2025 is a month of deep intimacy, emotional healing, and spiritual growth. With Venus, the planet of love and relationships, entering your 12th house of spirituality, surrender, and unconditional love on September 19th, you may feel a strong desire for a soul-level connection with your partner or a divine love that transcends the physical realm. This is a fantastic time to deepen your existing relationship through shared spiritual practices, emotional vulnerability, and acts of selfless service, or to attract a new partnership that is based on mutual growth, healing, and unconditional love. Trust your heart and be open to giving and receiving love in all its forms, even if it means facing your deepest fears, wounds, or shadows.

If you're in a committed relationship, take time to explore the deeper layers of your connection, such as your shared values, beliefs, and spiritual path. Be willing to be vulnerable and transparent about your hopes, fears, and dreams, and to support your partner's growth and healing with love, compassion, and understanding. Remember that true intimacy requires both partners to show up fully and authentically, and to create a safe space for emotional and spiritual growth.

If you're single, you may attract people who share your depth, sensitivity, and spiritual values. Look for partners who are willing to do the inner work of growth and transformation, and who appreciate your unique gifts and strengths. Trust your intuition and take your time getting to know potential partners before jumping into a serious relationship. Remember that the most important relationship is the one you have with yourself and the divine, and that self-love and spiritual connection are essential for attracting healthy, fulfilling partnerships.

Career:

In your career, September 2025 is a month of power, ambition, and personal achievement. With

Mars entering your sign on September 22nd, you may feel a strong drive to pursue your professional goals, take on new challenges, and assert your leadership skills and expertise. This is a fantastic time to start a new project, launch a business venture, or go after a promotion or raise. Trust your instincts and be willing to take bold, decisive action towards your dreams and aspirations, even if it means stepping outside your comfort zone or taking risks.

On September 21st, the New Moon in Virgo coincides with a Partial Solar Eclipse, bringing a powerful new beginning or fresh start in your 11th house of friendships, networking, and community. This is an excellent time to expand your social connections, join a professional organization or group, or collaborate with like-minded individuals who share your values, interests, and goals. Trust that the universe is guiding you towards the right people and opportunities that will support your growth and success, and be open to giving and receiving help and support along the way.

Finances:

In finances, September 2025 is a month of abundance, prosperity, and positive change. With Jupiter, the planet of expansion and abundance, forming a trine aspect to the True Node in your 6th house of work and service on September 3rd, you may experience financial rewards, opportunities, or breakthroughs related to your job, business, or investments. Trust that your efforts, skills, and talents are being recognized and valued, and that the universe is supporting your financial growth and success.

On September 11th, Saturn, your traditional ruler, turns direct in your 4th house of home, family, and emotional foundations. This transit may bring a period of stability, structure, and long-term planning in your financial life, particularly related to real estate, property, or family investments. You may need to take a more disciplined, responsible approach to your finances, and to make sure that your spending and saving habits align with your values, goals, and long-term security. Trust your inner wisdom and be open to making necessary adjustments or sacrifices that will pay off in the long run.

Health:

In health, September 2025 is a month of deep healing, self-care, and inner transformation. With the Full Moon in Pisces on September 7th coinciding with a Total Lunar Eclipse in your 5th house of self-expression and joy, you may experience a powerful release or breakthrough in your physical, emotional, or spiritual well-being. This is a fantastic time to let go of old patterns, habits, or beliefs that are no longer serving your highest good, and to embrace a new level of self-love, creativity, and vitality. Trust the process of renewal and regeneration, and know that you have the power to create a healthy, vibrant, and fulfilling life.

On September 22nd, Mars enters your sign, bringing a surge of energy, motivation, and vitality to your health and well-being. Use this transit to establish healthy habits, routines, and self-care practices that support your physical, emotional, and spiritual health, such as regular exercise, nutritious eating, and stress-management techniques. Trust your body's innate wisdom and be open to making necessary changes or adjustments that allow you to feel your best and thrive.

Travel:

In travel, September 2025 may bring opportunities for spiritual pilgrimages, retreats, or soul-searching journeys. With Venus entering your 12th house of spirituality, surrender, and inner growth on September 19th, you may feel called to visit sacred sites, connect with nature, or explore new spiritual practices and traditions that deepen your connection with the divine and your inner wisdom. Consider taking a trip to a peaceful, serene location such as a monastery, ashram, or natural wonder, where you can unplug from the outside world and tune into your inner guidance and intuition.

If travel isn't possible or practical, find ways to bring a sense of inner exploration, self-discovery, and spiritual growth into your daily life. Engage in practices such as meditation, prayer, or dream work that allow you to access your subconscious mind and connect with a higher power or purpose. Remember that travel is not just about the destination, but about the journey of self-discovery, healing, and transformation.

Insights from the Stars:

The celestial energies of September 2025 remind you of the power of surrender, faith, and inner transformation. With the Full Moon in Pisces coinciding with a Total Lunar Eclipse in your 5th house of creativity, self-expression, and joy on September 7th, you are being called to let go of control, trust in the flow of life, and allow yourself to be guided by a higher power or purpose. This is a time to face your deepest fears, heal your deepest wounds, and connect with your authentic self and soul's calling.

On September 22nd, Mars enters your sign, bringing a powerful new beginning and fresh start in your personal growth, self-discovery, and self-empowerment. Trust your instincts, take bold action towards your goals, and know that the universe is supporting you every step of the way. Remember that you are a powerful creator and manifestor, and that your thoughts, beliefs, and actions shape your reality. Embrace your inner warrior, leader, and healer, and know that you have the power to transform your life and the world around you.

Best Days of the Month:

- September 3rd: Jupiter trine True Node - Financial rewards, opportunities, or breakthroughs related to your job, business, or investments, with a sense of purpose and fulfillment.
- September 7th: Full Moon in Pisces and Total Lunar Eclipse - A powerful culmination or turning point in your journey of creativity, self-expression, and joy, with opportunities for deep healing and transformation.
- September 19th: Venus enters 12th house - Opportunities for spiritual growth, unconditional love, and soul-level connections in your relationships and inner life.
- September 21st: New Moon in Virgo and Partial Solar Eclipse - A powerful new beginning or fresh start in your friendships, networking, and community involvement, with opportunities for collaboration and support.

- September 22nd: Mars enters Scorpio - A surge of energy, passion, and motivation to pursue your personal goals, assert your needs and desires, and make your mark on the world, with opportunities for growth and empowerment.

October 2025

Overview Horoscope for the Month:

Scorpio, October 2025 is a month of intense transformation, deep healing, and personal empowerment. As the heart of autumn and your birthday season, it brings a sense of rebirth, renewal, and new beginnings that will catalyze your evolution and self-discovery. Prepare to shed old skin, confront your shadows and fears, and emerge as a more authentic, powerful, and aligned version of yourself. Trust the journey and know that you have the strength, wisdom, and resilience to handle whatever comes your way.

The month starts with a powerful astrological event as Pluto, your modern ruler, turns direct in your 3rd house of communication, learning, and self-expression on October 13th. This transit, which has been retrograde since May 4th, will bring a sense of forward momentum, clarity, and empowerment to your mental and verbal abilities. You may feel a strong urge to speak your truth, share your knowledge and ideas, and assert your voice and influence in the world. Use this time to actively pursue your intellectual interests, engage in meaningful conversations and debates, and express yourself with confidence, conviction, and authenticity.

On October 21st, the New Moon in Libra falls in your 12th house of spirituality, surrender, and inner growth. This powerful lunation brings a new beginning or fresh start in your journey of emotional healing, spiritual awakening, and self-discovery. You may feel called to retreat from the world, engage in solitary practices such as meditation or journaling, and connect with your inner guidance and intuition. Trust the process of release and renewal, and know that you are being supported by the universe in your path of growth and transformation.

Love:

In love, October 2025 is a month of deep intimacy, emotional healing, and spiritual growth. With Venus, the planet of love and relationships, entering your sign on November 6th, you may feel a strong desire for passionate, intense, and transformative connections that challenge you to grow, evolve, and express your authentic self. This is a fantastic time to deepen your existing relationship through honest communication, vulnerability, and shared experiences, or to attract a new partnership that is based on mutual respect, trust, and growth. Trust your heart and be open to giving and receiving love in all its forms, even if it means facing your fears, wounds, or shadows.

If you're in a committed relationship, take time to explore the deeper layers of your connection, such as your shared values, goals, and long-term vision. Be willing to have difficult conversations, work through conflicts or challenges, and support each other's individual growth and evolution. Remember that true intimacy requires both partners to show up fully and authentically, and to create a safe space for emotional and spiritual growth.

If you're single, you may attract people who share your depth, intensity, and desire for transformation. Look for partners who are willing to do the inner work of healing and growth, and who appreciate your unique gifts, strengths, and challenges. Trust your intuition and take your time getting to know potential partners before jumping into a serious relationship. Remember that the most important relationship is the one you have with yourself, and that self-love and self-acceptance are essential for attracting healthy, fulfilling partnerships.

Career:

In your career, October 2025 is a month of power, ambition, and personal achievement. With Mars, your traditional ruler, traveling through your sign for the entire month, you may feel a strong drive to pursue your professional goals, take on new challenges, and assert your leadership skills and expertise. This is a fantastic time to start a new project, launch a business venture, or go after a promotion or raise. Trust your instincts and be willing to take bold, decisive action towards your dreams and aspirations, even if it means stepping outside your comfort zone or taking risks.

On October 27th, Jupiter, the planet of expansion and abundance, turns direct in your 10th house of career and public reputation. This transit, which has been retrograde since November 11th, will bring a sense of forward momentum, growth, and opportunity to your professional life. You may receive recognition, rewards, or new opportunities that align with your skills, talents, and long-term goals. Trust that the universe is supporting your success and fulfillment, and be open to new paths or directions that feel authentic and meaningful to you.

Finances:

In finances, October 2025 is a month of abundance, prosperity, and positive change. With Venus, the planet of love and money, entering your sign on November 6th, you may experience a surge of financial opportunities, rewards, or windfalls that align with your values, desires, and personal power. This is a fantastic time to assert your worth, negotiate for what you want, and make financial decisions that support your long-term security and abundance. Trust your instincts and be open to new sources of income or investments that feel authentic and empowering to you.

On October 16th, Mercury, the planet of communication and commerce, enters your sign, bringing a sense of mental clarity, focus, and persuasion to your financial dealings. Use this transit to actively pursue your financial goals, communicate your needs and desires, and make strategic decisions that align with your values and priorities. Remember that true wealth comes from a sense of inner abundance, gratitude, and purpose, and that money is simply a tool to support your dreams and aspirations.

Health:

In health, October 2025 is a month of deep healing, self-care, and inner transformation. With the New Moon in Libra on October 21st falling in your 12th house of spirituality and inner growth, you may feel a strong urge to retreat from the world, rest and recharge, and connect with your inner guidance and intuition. This is a fantastic time to engage in practices such as meditation, yoga, or energy healing that support your physical, emotional, and spiritual well-being, and to release any patterns, habits, or beliefs that are no longer serving your highest good.

On October 6th, Mars, your traditional ruler, forms a sextile aspect to Uranus in your 6th house of health and daily routines. This harmonious alignment brings opportunities for positive change, innovation, and breakthroughs in your self-care practices and lifestyle choices. You may feel inspired to try new forms of exercise, nutrition, or alternative therapies that support your vitality, energy, and overall well-being. Trust your body's innate wisdom and be open to making necessary changes or adjustments that allow you to feel your best and thrive.

Travel:
In travel, October 2025 may bring opportunities for personal growth, self-discovery, and inner exploration. With the New Moon in Libra on October 21st falling in your 12th house of spirituality and inner growth, you may feel called to take a solo retreat, attend a workshop or seminar, or visit a sacred site or natural wonder that allows you to connect with your inner wisdom and guidance. Consider taking a trip that focuses on emotional healing, spiritual awakening, or creative expression, such as a yoga retreat, art workshop, or nature immersion.

If travel isn't possible or practical, find ways to bring a sense of inner exploration, self-discovery, and growth into your daily life. Engage in practices such as journaling, dream work, or creative visualization that allow you to access your subconscious mind and connect with your authentic self and desires. Remember that travel is not just about the destination, but about the journey of self-discovery, healing, and transformation.

Insights from the Stars:

The celestial energies of October 2025 remind you of the power of authenticity, self-expression, and personal transformation. With Pluto turning direct in your 3rd house of communication and learning on October 13th, you are being called to speak your truth, share your knowledge and ideas, and assert your voice and influence in the world. This is a time to actively pursue your intellectual interests, engage in meaningful conversations and debates, and express yourself with confidence, conviction, and authenticity.

On October 23rd, Mars, your traditional ruler, forms a square aspect to Pluto in your 3rd house, bringing intense power struggles, conflicts, or confrontations in your communication, learning, or self-expression. You may need to confront deep-seated fears, wounds, or limitations that are holding you back from fully expressing your authentic self and desires, or to engage in difficult conversations or negotiations that challenge your beliefs, values, or sense of power. Trust your inner strength and wisdom, and know that the challenges you face are ultimately serving your growth, healing, and transformation.

Best Days of the Month:

- October 6th: Mars sextile Uranus - Opportunities for positive change, innovation, and breakthroughs in your health, self-care, and daily routines.
- October 13th: Pluto turns direct in 3rd house - Forward momentum, clarity, and empowerment in your communication, learning, and self-expression.
- October 16th: Mercury enters Scorpio - Mental clarity, focus, and persuasion in your personal goals, desires, and financial dealings.
- October 21st: New Moon in Libra - A new beginning or fresh start in your journey of emotional healing, spiritual awakening, and self-discovery.
- October 27th: Jupiter turns direct in 10th house - Forward momentum, growth, and opportunity in your career, public reputation, and long-term goals.

November 2025

Overview Horoscope for the Month:

Scorpio, November 2025 is a month of intense transformation, deep healing, and personal empowerment. As the final month of autumn and the peak of your birthday season, it brings a sense of culmination, completion, and new beginnings that will catalyze your evolution and self-discovery. Prepare to shed old patterns, beliefs, and limitations that no longer serve your highest good, and to embrace a new level of authenticity, power, and alignment with your soul's purpose. Trust the journey and know that you have the strength, wisdom, and resilience to handle whatever comes your way.

The month starts with a powerful astrological event as Venus, the planet of love and relationships, enters your sign on November 6th. This transit, which lasts until November 30th, will bring a surge of magnetic attraction, personal charisma, and romantic opportunities to your life. You may feel more confident, alluring, and ready to pursue your heart's desires and attract the love, pleasure, and abundance you deserve. Use this time to focus on your self-love, self-care, and self-expression, and to surround yourself with beauty, art, and sensual delights that nourish your soul.

On November 28th, the New Moon in Sagittarius falls in your 2nd house of values, resources, and self-worth. This powerful lunation brings a new beginning or fresh start in your journey of financial abundance, personal empowerment, and self-esteem. You may feel called to reassess your priorities, values, and beliefs around money and success, and to align your resources and talents with your authentic self and purpose. Trust the process of manifestation and attraction, and know that you have the power to create a life of prosperity, fulfillment, and joy.

Love:

In love, November 2025 is a month of deep intimacy, emotional healing, and spiritual growth. With Venus traveling through your sign for most of the month, you may feel a strong desire for passionate, intense, and transformative connections that challenge you to grow, evolve, and express your authentic self. This is a fantastic time to deepen your existing relationship through honest communication, vulnerability, and shared experiences, or to attract a new partnership that is based on mutual respect, trust, and growth. Trust your heart and be open to giving and receiving love in all its forms, even if it means facing your fears, wounds, or shadows.

If you're in a committed relationship, take time to explore the deeper layers of your connection, such as your shared values, goals, and long-term vision. Be willing to have difficult conversations, work through conflicts or challenges, and support each other's individual growth and evolution. Remember that true intimacy requires both partners to show up fully and authentically, and to create a safe space for emotional and spiritual growth.

If you're single, you may attract people who share your depth, intensity, and desire for transformation. Look for partners who are willing to do the inner work of healing and growth, and who appreciate your unique gifts, strengths, and challenges. Trust your intuition and take your time getting to know potential partners before jumping into a serious relationship. Remember that the most important relationship is the one you have with yourself, and that self-love and self-acceptance are essential for attracting healthy, fulfilling partnerships.

Career:

In your career, November 2025 is a month of success, recognition, and personal achievement. With Mars, your traditional ruler, traveling through your 2nd house of values and resources until November 4th, you may feel a strong drive to pursue your financial goals, assert your worth, and make strategic decisions that support your long-term security and success. This is a fantastic time to negotiate a raise or promotion, start a side hustle or business venture, or invest in your skills and talents. Trust your instincts and be willing to take bold, decisive action towards your dreams and aspirations, even if it means stepping outside your comfort zone or taking risks.

On November 9th, Mercury, the planet of communication and commerce, turns retrograde in your 2nd house of values and resources. This transit, which lasts until November 29th, may bring a period of reflection, re-evaluation, and inner growth around your financial beliefs, habits, and strategies. You may need to review your budget, investments, or spending patterns, and to make necessary adjustments or changes that align with your authentic values and priorities. Trust your inner wisdom and be open to new perspectives or insights that can help you create a more abundant, fulfilling, and purposeful financial life.

Finances:

In finances, November 2025 is a month of abundance, prosperity, and positive change. With the New Moon in Sagittarius on November 28th falling in your 2nd house of values and resources, you may experience a powerful new beginning or fresh start in your journey of financial empowerment, self-worth, and manifestation. This is a fantastic time to set intentions, affirm your abundance, and take inspired action towards your financial goals and dreams. Trust that the universe is conspiring to support your success and fulfillment, and be open to unexpected opportunities or synchronicities that align with your highest good.

On November 12th, Saturn, your traditional ruler, turns direct in your 4th house of home, family, and emotional foundations. This transit, which has been retrograde since July 13th, will bring a sense of stability, structure, and forward momentum to your financial life, particularly related to real estate, property, or family investments. You may need to take a more disciplined, responsible approach to your finances, and to make sure that your spending and saving habits align with your values, goals, and long-term security. Trust your inner wisdom and be open to making necessary adjustments or sacrifices that will pay off in the long run.

Health:

In health, November 2025 is a month of deep healing, self-care, and inner transformation. With Neptune, the planet of spirituality and unconditional love, traveling through your 5th house of creativity, joy, and self-expression, you may feel a strong urge to engage in practices that nourish your soul, uplift your spirit, and connect you with a sense of divine love and grace. This is a fantastic time to explore artistic pursuits, romantic adventures, or playful activities that bring you a sense of joy, wonder, and inspiration, and to release any patterns, habits, or beliefs that are blocking your natural vitality and radiance.

On November 7th, Pluto, your modern ruler, forms a semi-square aspect to the True Node in your 5th house of creativity and self-expression. This challenging alignment may bring up deep fears, wounds, or limitations around your ability to fully express your authentic self and desires, or to connect with a sense of purpose and meaning in your life. You may need to confront patterns of self-doubt, shame, or repression that are holding you back from your true potential and joy. Trust your inner strength and wisdom, and know that the challenges you face are ultimately serving your growth, healing, and transformation.

Travel:

In travel, November 2025 may bring opportunities for adventure, learning, and personal growth. With Venus traveling through your sign for most of the month, you may feel a strong desire to explore new places, cultures, or experiences that expand your mind, heart, and soul. Consider taking a trip that focuses on beauty, art, or sensual pleasures, such as a wine-tasting tour, art museum visit, or spa retreat. Trust your instincts and be open to spontaneous detours or surprises that can lead to unexpected delights and discoveries.

If travel isn't possible or practical, find ways to bring a sense of adventure, curiosity, and growth into your daily life. Explore your local community or region with fresh eyes, attend cultural events or workshops, or connect with people from different backgrounds and perspectives. Remember that travel is not just about the destination, but about the journey of self-discovery, learning, and transformation.

Insights from the Stars:

The celestial energies of November 2025 remind you of the power of self-love, self-worth, and personal empowerment. With Venus traveling through your sign for most of the month, you are being called to embrace your unique beauty, talents, and desires, and to attract the love, abundance, and joy you deserve. This is a time to focus on your self-care, self-expression, and self-acceptance, and to surround yourself with people, experiences, and environments that reflect your authentic self and values.

On November 17th, Jupiter, the planet of expansion and growth, forms a sesquadrate aspect to Pluto in your 3rd house of communication and learning. This challenging alignment may bring up intense power struggles, conflicts, or confrontations in your relationships, interactions, or intellectual pursuits. You may need to confront deep-seated fears, wounds, or limitations that are holding you back from fully expressing your truth and wisdom, or to engage in difficult conversations or negotiations that challenge your beliefs, values, or sense of authority. Trust your inner strength and integrity, and know that the challenges you face are ultimately serving your growth, healing, and transformation.

Best Days of the Month:

- November 6th: Venus enters Scorpio - A surge of magnetic attraction, personal charisma, and romantic opportunities in your life, with a focus on self-love, self-care, and self-expression.
- November 12th: Saturn turns direct in 4th house - Forward momentum, stability, and structure in your financial life, particularly related to real estate, property, or family investments.
- November 25th: Venus conjunct Jupiter in Scorpio - Abundant blessings, opportunities, and positive energy in your love life, finances, and personal growth.

- November 28th: New Moon in Sagittarius - A powerful new beginning or fresh start in your journey of financial empowerment, self-worth, and manifestation.
- November 30th: Venus enters Sagittarius - Expansive, optimistic, and adventurous energy in your love life, creativity, and self-expression, with opportunities for travel, learning, and personal growth.

December 2025

Overview Horoscope for the Month:

Scorpio, December 2025 is a month of deep introspection, emotional healing, and spiritual growth. As the final month of the year, it brings a sense of closure, completion, and new beginnings that will catalyze your evolution and self-discovery. Prepare to dive deep into your psyche, confront your shadows and fears, and emerge with a renewed sense of purpose, power, and alignment with your soul's path. Trust the journey and know that you are exactly where you need to be.

The month starts with a powerful astrological event as Neptune, the planet of spirituality and transcendence, turns direct in your 5th house of creativity, self-expression, and joy on December 10th. This transit, which has been retrograde since July 4th, will bring a sense of clarity, inspiration, and forward momentum to your artistic pursuits, romantic life, and personal fulfillment. You may feel a strong urge to express your authentic self, explore your imagination and intuition, and connect with a higher power or purpose. Use this time to actively pursue your passions, nurture your inner child, and embrace the magic and wonder of life.

On December 19th, the New Moon in Sagittarius falls in your 2nd house of values, resources, and self-worth. This powerful lunation brings a new beginning or fresh start in your journey of financial abundance, personal empowerment, and self-esteem. You may feel called to reassess your priorities, values, and beliefs around money and success, and to align your resources and talents with your authentic self and purpose. Trust the process of manifestation and attraction, and know that you have the power to create a life of prosperity, fulfillment, and joy.

Love:

In love, December 2025 is a month of deep intimacy, emotional healing, and spiritual growth. With Venus, the planet of love and relationships, joining Pluto in your 3rd house of communication and self-expression, you may feel a strong desire for honest, authentic, and transformative connections that challenge you to grow, evolve, and express your truth. This is a fantastic time to have deep, meaningful conversations with your partner, to share your innermost thoughts and feelings, and to create a safe space for vulnerability and trust. Trust your heart and be open to giving and receiving love in all its forms, even if it means facing your fears, wounds, or shadows.

If you're in a committed relationship, take time to explore the power of words, both spoken and unspoken, in your connection. Be willing to listen deeply, communicate openly, and support each other's growth and healing through honest, compassionate dialogue. Remember that true intimacy requires both partners to show up fully and authentically, and to create a safe space for emotional and spiritual growth.

If you're single, you may attract people who share your depth, intensity, and desire for meaningful communication. Look for partners who are willing to engage in deep, authentic conversations, and who appreciate your unique perspective, insights, and wisdom. Trust your intuition and take your time getting to know potential partners before jumping into a serious relationship. Remember that the most important relationship is the one you have with yourself, and that self-love and self-acceptance are essential for attracting healthy, fulfilling partnerships.

Career:

In your career, December 2025 is a month of innovation, progress, and positive change. With Mars, your traditional ruler, entering Capricorn on December 15th, you may feel a strong drive to pursue your professional goals, take on new responsibilities, and assert your leadership skills and expertise. This is a fantastic time to focus on your long-term career vision, to set ambitious yet realistic goals, and to take practical, strategic action towards your dreams and aspirations. Trust your instincts and be willing to put in the hard work and dedication required for success, even if it means facing challenges or obstacles along the way.

On December 11th, Mercury, the planet of communication and commerce, enters Capricorn, bringing a sense of mental clarity, focus, and discipline to your professional endeavors. Use this transit to actively pursue your career goals, communicate your ideas and plans, and make strategic decisions that align with your values and priorities. Remember that success is not just about achieving external milestones, but also about finding a sense of purpose, fulfillment, and inner satisfaction in your work.

Finances:

In finances, December 2025 is a month of abundance, prosperity, and positive change. With the

New Moon in Sagittarius on December 19th falling in your 2nd house of values and resources, you may experience a powerful new beginning or fresh start in your journey of financial empowerment, self-worth, and manifestation. This is a fantastic time to set intentions, affirm your abundance, and take inspired action towards your financial goals and dreams. Trust that the universe is conspiring to support your success and fulfillment, and be open to unexpected opportunities or synchronicities that align with your highest good.

On December 21st, Jupiter, the planet of expansion and abundance, forms a square aspect to Chiron in your 6th house of work, health, and service. This challenging alignment may bring up wounds, insecurities, or limitations around your ability to manifest abundance through your daily work and routines, or to find a sense of purpose and fulfillment in your financial life. You may need to confront patterns of self-doubt, scarcity, or over-giving that are holding you back from true prosperity and self-care. Trust your inner wisdom and be open to making necessary adjustments or boundaries that align with your highest values and long-term goals.

Health:

In health, December 2025 is a month of vitality, energy, and inner growth. With the Sun, the planet of life force and vitality, entering your 3rd house of communication and learning on December 21st, you may feel a renewed sense of curiosity, mental clarity, and desire for knowledge and understanding. This is a fantastic time to engage in practices that stimulate your mind, expand your perspective, and keep you mentally sharp and agile, such as reading, writing, or learning a new skill or language. Trust that your mind-body connection is a powerful tool for overall health and well-being.

On December 26th, Uranus, the planet of sudden change and innovation, turns direct in your 7th house of partnerships and one-on-one relationships. This transit may bring unexpected shifts, breakthroughs, or awakenings in your closest connections, particularly around issues of freedom, individuality, and authenticity. You may need to confront patterns of codependency, power struggles, or limiting beliefs that are holding you back from true intimacy and growth. Trust your inner wisdom and be open to making necessary changes or adjustments that allow you to express your true self and create relationships that support your highest good.

Travel:

In travel, December 2025 may bring opportunities for spiritual growth, inner exploration, and connection with nature. With Neptune turning direct in your 5th house of creativity and self-expression on December 10th, you may feel a strong urge to visit beautiful, inspiring places that allow you to tap into your imagination, intuition, and sense of wonder. Consider taking a trip to a serene, natural setting, such as a beach, forest, or mountain retreat, where you can unplug from technology, slow down, and immerse yourself in the healing energy of the earth.

If travel isn't possible or practical, find ways to bring a sense of beauty, inspiration, and spiritual connection into your daily life. Engage in creative activities that allow you to express your unique talents and gifts, spend time in nature or with animals, or seek out experiences that uplift your soul and remind you of the magic and mystery of life. Remember that travel is not just about the destination, but about the journey of self-discovery, healing, and transformation.

Insights from the Stars:

The celestial energies of December 2025 remind you of the power of communication, self-expression, and spiritual growth. With Venus joining Pluto in your

3rd house of communication and learning, you are being called to speak your truth, share your knowledge and wisdom, and engage in meaningful conversations and connections that support your growth and transformation. This is a time to actively pursue your intellectual and creative interests, to express yourself with confidence and authenticity, and to trust in the power of words to heal, inspire, and create positive change.

On December 28th, Mercury, the planet of communication and learning, enters Aquarius, bringing a sense of innovation, originality, and social awareness to your mental pursuits and interactions. You may feel a strong urge to connect with like-minded individuals who share your values, ideals, and vision for the future, or to use your voice and influence to make a positive impact in your community or the world at large. Trust your unique perspective and insights, and know that your ideas and contributions have the power to create meaningful change and progress.

Best Days of the Month:

- December 10th: Neptune turns direct in 5th house - Forward momentum, clarity, and

inspiration in your creativity, self-expression, and spiritual growth.
- December 19th: New Moon in Sagittarius - A powerful new beginning or fresh start in your journey of financial empowerment, self-worth, and manifestation.
- December 21st: Sun enters 3rd house - Renewed curiosity, mental clarity, and desire for knowledge and understanding in your communication and learning.
- December 26th: Uranus turns direct in 7th house - Unexpected shifts, breakthroughs, or awakenings in your closest relationships that support your growth and authenticity.
- December 28th: Mercury enters Aquarius - Innovative, original, and socially aware energy in your mental pursuits and interactions, with opportunities for positive change and progress.